GW00480701

THE CORNISH JOURNAL, 1892–1908

of

CHARLES LEE

THE CORNISH JOURNAL

of

CHARLES LEE

Edited by

K. C. Phillipps

TABB HOUSE

Padstow

First published 1995
Tabb House, 7 Church Street, Padstow, Cornwall, PL28 8BG

ISBN 0 907018 97 1 – hardback
ISBN 1 873951 09 4 – paperback

British Library Cataloguing-in-Publication Data:
A catalogue record of this title is available from the
British Library.

Typeset by Exe Valley Dataset
and printed by Short Run Press, Exeter

Books by K. C. Phillipps

Jane Austen's English
Westcountry Words and Ways
The Language of Thackeray
Language and Class in Victorian England
A Glossary of the Cornish Dialect
Catching Cornwall in Flight
   or the Bettermost Class of People

For John and Constance Rowe

CONTENTS

LIST OF ILLUSTRATIONS

ACKNOWLEDGEMENTS

My first and greatest debt is to Mr G. Jones of Letchworth, who made Charles Lee's five little note-books available to me.

I also wish to thank Mr R. Penhallurick, Senior Curator, Royal Cornwall Museum, for a great deal of help in choosing suitable photographs and the Royal Institute of Cornwall for permission to reproduce them.

K. C. Phillipps

INTRODUCTION

Charles Lee was a Londoner, born in 1870. He attended Highgate School, and eventually graduated from London University. Perhaps partly for health reasons, in 1893 he went to live for a time in Green Street, Newlyn, staying with a Mr and Mrs Simons, who owned a fishing boat. For most of the time that he was in Cornwall he kept a Journal, eventually five note-books, full of observations on folk-lore, on sociology (though the word was hardly in use) and also on local speech.

In those days Cornwall had not yet been 'discovered', to use Sir Arthur Quiller-Couch's word. Yet Newlyn was not exactly a typically remote Cornish fishing village; there was a thriving and relatively sophisticated artists' colony, who painted the fisherfolk and Cornish scenes, in the open air. Lee, whose status as a 'gentleman' was recognised locally, gained admission to these artistic circles, partly by being a good pianist. He was in demand as an accompanist for the concerts they gave. Soon Lee was rubbing shoulders with men whose fame as artists is now secure: Stanhope Forbes, Frank Bramley, Walter Langley and 'Lamorna' Birch. Being perhaps slightly Bohemian, these men were very approachable; and Lee frequently dined at the home of the painter and book-illustrator T.C. Gotch. At a Christmas party at Stanhope Forbes' studio, he met Miss

Margaret Courtney, and noted not only that she was the sister of Leonard Courtney, MP, but also that she was the author of a glossary of West Cornwall words. At Christmas time, too, back at his 'lodge' (to use the dialect word), there would be ghost stories from Mrs Simons, which Lee clearly half believed.

When Lee writes in his Journal 'work up' or 'might make something of this', he means that he intends to use his notes for a forthcoming novel. For this was his chosen career. By the end of the century he had three books to his credit: *Paul Carah Cornishman* (1898), *The Widow Woman* (1899) and *Cynthia in the West* (1900).

From the Journal it is not possible now to track down how long Lee stayed in the various places he chose to live: Cadgwith, Portloe, etc. After less than a year references to Newlyn cease; and there were frequent returns to London. He seems to have found it difficult to collect material in the relaxed atmosphere of Cornwall, while writing for a critical London audience. In Portloe, which must have been really remote in the eighteen-nineties, he ruminates: 'Living as one likes . . . is it good for any of us? Is there one of us who does not need the social restraint . . . the clean collar every day?' (Even in Portloe, he tells us, the young men wore clean collars to chapel on Sundays.)

There is a greater antiquarian awareness, and also a more fluent polish, in the last two of the five volumes of the Journal, which deal chiefly with Lee's stay in the village of Mawgan-in-Pydar. By this time a married man, he remained several months in 'Mawgan', as he calls it, in 1903. The place seems to have won his heart . . . he called his Finchley house Lanherne, and the house in Letchworth where he eventually died, Lanvean: both Mawgan names. He entered fully into Mawgan life while there; being, among other things, church organist and choirmaster. Not being a native of Cornwall, he had none of the inhibitions current at the time about teetotalism; and no doubt many of the 'yarns', the tall stories and reminiscences, emanated from the Falcon Inn in the village. Nevertheless, his great friend, Reuben Rosevear, pre-eminently good at 'telling the tale', was not a drinker. At any rate, the latter part of *Our Little Town* (1909) and the whole of *Dorinda's Birthday* (1911) are set in Mawgan.

And then there were no more novels. Sir Arthur Quiller-Couch, who produced a selection of Lee's writing entitled *Cornish Tales*, in 1941, writes in the Introduction that probably 'the ill-success of *Dorinda* may have discouraged Mr Lee, 'too quick despairer', from further writing. *Dorinda's Birthday*, Q thought, was 'a masterpiece'; and again, we can see Lee 'working up'from the Journal set-pieces like the bell-ringing into a crucial event in the story.

In one respect, it is generally agreed, Lee's technique was masterly. It is clear from many entries in the Journal that he had made a close study of our dialect. To quote A.L. Rowse in *A Cornish Childhood*: 'The outsider who has come nearest to getting [our dialect] right is Charles Lee in his *Cornish Tales*; it is very remarkable, there is hardly a thing that one would question in his usage.' In thirty years time, when the dialect of Cornwall is finally dead, there may well be those who will want to read *The Widow Woman* for West Cornwall, and *Dorinda's Birthday* for mid-Cornwall, to know the way in which their ancestors spoke.

But already, by the publication of his last novel, Lee had

obtained a secure job with the publishers J.M. Dent of Letchworth; and he lived there, with occasional holidays in Cornwall, for the rest of his life. He died at the age of eighty-six in 1956; his last major publication being the often-reprinted anthology of bad verse, *The Stuffed Owl*, with D.B. Wyndham Lewis, in 1930. He lived long enough to see a one-act play of his, *Mr Sampson*, performed for television.

The claims of Lee's little Journal on our attention will be obvious on brief perusal. As we say in Cornwall 'He don't miss much'. As a reader and proof-reader in Letchworth, he had a reputation for 'knowing everything'; and he brings to the Cornwall he experienced a sharp observation and a great fund of literary and antiquarian knowledge. He loved talking to the elderly; from them, for instance, he caught glimpses of what smuggling was like in its heyday, and wrecking; he learnt of the cholera outbreak in Mevagissey in 1849, and noted down changes in farming methods. This little book is worthy to stand alongside that classic of Devon reminiscence, Cecil Torr's *Small Talk at Wreyland*.

1. Pencil drawing of Lee, 1908, aged 38

1892–1893
Newlyn

November 22nd, 1892. Wind N.W. fresh. The boats were out last night; brought in 3,500 herring; but herring are only a shilling a hundred today, owing to a big catch by a couple of boats who let down a seine outside Penzance. This, I understand, is a very unusual way of catching herring. Sometimes they are as much as 2s. 6d. or 3s. a hundred. The boat carries one share, the owners of the nets one, the captain one and the men who give their labour only take half a share. Mrs Simons handles three shares, one for the boat, one for the nets and one for Mr S. as captain. Mr S. declares he would rather go whaling or to the workhouse than belong to the North Sea fleet. The grievance is that the men are not their own masters, and by their agreement with the owners of the boats they are obliged to remain out for six weeks at a time – in all weathers. If they run back they are dismissed. A smack like the Simons' costs about £300 to build and lasts thirty or forty years. The boats now built are much swifter than the old ones: on the approach of bad weather they generally manage to reach land, and are seldom obliged to have recourse to 'rafting'.

The 'churchtowns' hereabouts have each an annual 'feast-day', when all friends and relations from neighbouring villages are invited to sup, and merry-making is the rule.

Mr Simons's dream is to live inland. 'That's where I'd like to live, Muster Lee, 'mong the trees, where nothin'd meet my sight but trees. Out o' sight o' the say for ever.' He tells a jape current here concerning Paddy, who put his candle into the oven to dry it: 'The more it's dry, the more it's wet,' said Paddy.

The people here do not marry with other districts. But at St Ives mixed marriages, especially with East countryfolk, seem more common.

A tight cobbin' is a good hiding.

November 25th. In the morning when the sun is shining down the street as I lie on the sofa and look out of the window, a bright reflection is cast from the person of every passer-by upon the ceiling. The men have been passing up and down this morning, carrying golden brown nets and oars and other gear, and barrels of water, and sacks and baskets of potatoes and turnips and bread and meal to victual their boat for the week. A crew of six men take a quarter of a hundredweight of meat for a week's provision. The boat went off this morning for Plymouth and is to remain there until a fortnight after Christmas. The boats going to Plymouth take a week's provision, including a hundredweight of bread or biscuit, meat as aforesaid, tea, groceries, etc. They travel by night as well as by day. The journey yesterday was expected to take twenty-four hours. About six years ago under very favourable circumstances the boats went from Newlyn to Whitby in three days; but it often takes a fortnight.

The old wrecking habits are not yet eradicated in Land's End. During the storm several vessels came ashore in Carbis Bay, and the people reaped a rich harvest of sofas and chairs and chests and firewood. But the law interfered and several were arrested. One old man of seventy who is reported to have been a wrecker by profession in the old days, was seen by a friend, toiling homeward under a big load of planks and spars. The friend warned him that the police were on the alert. He replied that he had permission, but showed manifest signs of fright. A little while afterwards he was found lying outside his door, dead, with the load still on him. The burden and the fright had affected his heart.

It is considered the proper thing here for a widower to marry again. Indeed, unless he has an unmarried daughter or other female relative it is a matter of necessity, especially if he has sons. There must be a woman in the house. Widowers seldom remain single more than a year.*

Mrs Simons cooked us some ling for dinner today – salted ling. There is a Cornish saying, apparently, 'tough as ling'. Heaven preserve us in future from salted ling.

November 30th. Lizzie off mending nets. The needles for netting are of two kinds: the *breeding* needle ('what we do breedie with' – notice the Cornish infinitive); this is used in making nets; and the *beeting* needle('what we do beetie with') used for mending. The former is made of some light-coloured flexible wood about ten inches long. When *breeding* a store of some twenty is kept ready at hand, fitted

*This is the theme of Lee's novel *The Widow Woman*.

2. Newlyn: the Cliff

with twine. The men make these needles themselves. The other, or *beating* needle, is smaller, say six inches, and made of bone. *Breeding* is going out of fashion, as machine-made nets are cheaper. The women who go out *beeting* get a shilling a day. However, hand-made rope is still the only use. It is in every way superior to the machine-made article. There is a rope-walk here under the Croft by the quarry, another opposite the St Just Road, and another at Street-an-Nowan.

December 2nd. News comes from Mousehole that when one of the boats was wearing to pass St Clement's Isle as it went into the harbour, the cargo of herrings shifted and the boat filled and went down at once. The men had only just time to jump into the punt and cut the rope. Three hundred pounds lost. By club rules members are entitled to two-thirds value if the loss is not less than ten pounds.

December 3rd. Old John B. who died last Saturday at over eighty was a great rascal. It was he who tried to grab the Green some years ago. The Green, an open space to the left of this house, is common land. He also went to law with a neighbour about a boundary wall, lost the suit and had to pay £30. In revenge, the old rogue one night climbed over the *ellins* (slates) and stopped up the chimneys of his opponents' 'barking house'. When they lit the fires and began to bark next morning, the house was filled with smoke, and work was impossible. After two or three days they ripped up the chimney, and halfway down found a frying-pan and a number of old bricks and rubbish.

In one of the houses along the cliff there is a woman, Mrs T., with two sons, who are both idiots, or 'big-headed', as they say here. According to Mrs Simons, the father courted another girl for some years and then went off and married the present Mrs T. In revenge, the rejected damsel 'wished' against her rival – 'wished her all kinds of things' says Mrs S. Only witchcraft, in the judgment of the village, is sufficient to account for such an awful misfortune.

When knitting, the needles not in use are stuck in a wisp of hay, bound round with threads and fastened at the waist. This is called a 'knitting sheet'.

A pig-sty is called a *pigs'-crow*, pronounced as *how*.

To come downstairs is to come *over stairs*.

To *garm* is to yell or shriek.

Mrs Simons tells how her father was once taken with bleeding at the nose. The doctors were called in, but could do nothing. He bled about a gallon of blood, and naturally began to feel very weak. He was preparing for death, when somebody thought of a famous charm doctor at Plymouth.

There was no time to send for the wizard; so they sent a telegram, asking him to charm father's nose at once. He did so and the bleeding stopped. This was thirty years ago, but it is quite a *fin-de-siècle* idea – ordering a spell by telegram – worthy of W.T. Stead.*

December 8th. In the afternoon, went to the Gotches'. Met Percy Craft** and Mrs Garstin.

December 9th. Mr Bolitho's wedding day.† Newlyn *en fête* with flags.

A lecture on ghosts by Mrs Simons last night. She believes in no ghosts but such as appear just when the breath of the departed 'do leave the body'. The theory is that a dead person can only appear before he or she has gone to the place appointed. Once they are in heaven they have no wish to return. If it is the other place they can't return if they wish. But in the interval, it is only reasonable to suppose that they may take the opportunity of visiting dear friends. For example, when Mrs Simons' mother died, one of her sons-in-law, who was very fond of her, was with the boat at Plymouth. The morning after her death, before the news was known, he told his mates that while lying in his bunk during the night, he felt 'Mother Jenny's' hand pass over his face.

Of wraiths of persons living it is said that if one is seen

*W.T. Stead (1849–1912) was an early exponent of stunt journalism.
**This Newlyn artist (1856–1934) was keen on amateur dramatics. The hospitable T.C.Gotch (1854–1931) was an artist and book illustrator.
†This was Thomas Bedford Bolitho, JP, MP for the St Ives division. The bride was Frances Jane Carus-Wilson, of Penmount, near Truro.

'when the days do lengthen' it portends a long life to the person whose semblance it wears, but if seen 'when the days do shorten', an early death is indicated.

Once, in her girlhood, Mrs Simons was coming home over Chun hill with a party of maidens, when they saw what seemed to be a carriage-light approaching up the road. They stepped aside to let it pass, but though they waited and listened, nothing passed them, and they heard no sound of wheels. They bolted, and ran all the way to the village. This was supposed to be one of the 'tin lights', seen hovering over a lode of tin.

Minnam = a little girl.

December 10th. Last night tar-barrels were lighted and coloured fires burnt. Candles in all the windows on the front, and 'ducks' or kettles of naphtha hanging from the cliff rails. I saw all this from Penzance parade. While the village was lighting up, and these lurid spots of fire were appearing in quick succession, Venus suddenly came out of a cloud over the hill-crest and looked on, brighter and larger and more lustrous than I ever saw her. Her track on the water was wide and bright and pure, flanked by the yellow and orange paths from the cressets on the pier.

Last night at the Gotches again. Met Mr and Mrs Stanhope Forbes*. He is littlish, slight and dark, with clear-cut aquiline features, something like Charles Lamb. He gesticulates when talking, and his talk is copious, discursive and – a little wearisome. He tells stories with all the

---

*This man (1857–1947) was very much the doyen of the Newlyn artists' colony. He specialised in large pictures of open-air subjects.

excessive detail of a charwoman. Very pleasant, though, and so is his wife. He brought his 'cello, and we had some songs by Mr and Mrs Gotch, etc. Mrs Craft was there. Mr Forbes tells how once coming home from somewhere late at night, he came across a dame with her head out of window conversing with a knot of people. They called him and asked him to lend his lantern, as they thought someone had fallen over the cliff. Making enquiries, he found that the dame had heard someone fall over half-an-hour before and had heard his groans ever since. She never woke her husband or attempted to call for assistance, though she stopped some people as they passed, to tell them the news. They were afraid to go down, as they hadn't a lantern, and hadn't the sense to go and find one. Forbes went down at once, and found a drunken man, lying on the rocks and groaning. Then he asked one of the young men to run into Penzance for Dr Simmons. The fellow refused: he was afraid to pass along Street-an-Nowan in the dark. Another lad was found to go with him.

Another story is of a young man in one of the smacks who received such a shock at having to hold up a drowning man over the boat side that he went out of his mind and is now in an asylum. And once there was a wreck off the Isle of Wight. The smacks were passing, bound for Whitby, and though the sea was not very rough, and the shipwrecked men were swimming and drowning before their eyes, they made no attempt to save them. They were simply paralysed with nervous excitement. Has the excessive quantity of tea they drink here anything to do with this neurotic temperament, which seems universal? Mr Gotch says that there have been several cases of men from the evening vessels

3. Artists' Studio, Newlyn

anchored at the pier, going on shore for groceries, stopping to have a glass or two, and starting back in the dark, half seas over, and then never seen or heard of again.

The boy talked of last night as Mrs Gotch's boy was an orphan whom the captain of a boat adopted. He was sent ashore with some message, and the captain gave him a shilling to spend as he liked. Boy-like, he spent it on sweets. He was a nice little fellow, and at the shops he visited he was full of the captain's kindness to him. The purchase of a shillingsworth of sweets was a matter of deliberation, occasioning, I suppose, much hanging about outside shop windows and at counters. What with one thing and another, he did not start for the boat till dark. It was a dirty night, and the quay is not safe walking at any time. He never reached the vessel. Next morning, Mrs Simons' nephew found his body washing about the harbour. Some of the sweets remained in his pocket.

Outside just now. Mrs Simons to neighbour starting for chapel: 'Gwine in 'long?' – 'In along' means towards the centre of the village; 'Out along' is the correlative. 'Down along' means towards the sea front, and 'Up along' means inland.

December 15th. At Christmas, I am told, boys and men go about the village in disguise, dancing and singing in the houses. They are called 'guise-dancers', with *guise* pronounced as in French.

The word for a well is *peeth*. A 'well' is a spring you go down to by steps.

Yesterday there was a funeral somewhere, and the village was full of folk in black. Everybody who can puts on mourning and goes to a funeral, even if they are totally unacquainted with the dead person. Grace Harvey never misses a funeral if she can help it. She is much distressed unless the funerals she attends are crowded with folk.

December 17th. Some local vocabulary and sayings:

spence a pantry

creen, as in *creening up*, complaining of illness, being a valetudinarian.

towzer, a large, rough apron

'She wished her cake dough and the pigs eating of it.'

An old man who had long been ailing died last night. His wife, a thriftless, dirty woman, the dirtiest woman in Newlyn, they say, is a most notorious beggar. This morning she and her sister locked the house up with the body inside it, and went off begging. People are speculating what will happen if the 'box' arrives at the deserted house today, and cannot be brought in.

December 19th. Mrs Simons says that the old sanded floors still exist up country and even here and there in the village. In her girlhood they were universal. They looked beautiful, she considers. The drawback was that the sand was carried about all over the house, into the chambers, etc., and also got into the food. People began to sand only round the room, under the furniture, leaving the middle bare. Others sanded only in the middle. Then they neglected to sand altogether.

Mrs Simon's friend, Mary Pollard, is built on the grand scale. She has a most dramatic delivery. She is sister-in-law to Ellen Garter, the dirtiest woman in Newlyn. Ellen was educated to be a lady. She can read and write 'lovely', play the piano and sew to perfection, but she was never brought up to work. Now, as Mrs Simons says, 'bring 'em up to work and you can make ladies of 'em afterwards, but bring 'em up to be ladies, and they'll never learn to work.'

Ellen G.'s children's clothes and her own were never washed. They were worn until they were dropping to pieces and saturated with grease. Then she would go into Penzance and buy some stuffs and set to work to make an apron or petticoat – as I said, she was an expert needle-woman. Then the old grease saturated garment was taken off and used to light the fire, and the new one put on. It used to be a joke: 'Ellen Garter's got a new apern. Old wan's gone to lightie the fire way.'

4. Fishwives, Newlyn *c*. 1900

December 24th. Mary Pollard's sister Elizabeth had her chap in one night and the old folk were gone to bed. It was getting late, so she and her lover climbed up, and put the clock back, but the clock had just struck ten. When the hands reached the hour again, it struck a second time. Elizabeth told Mary of this the next morning, and Mary shook her head. It was a 'token' as we all agreed. Elizabeth died soon after and, so far as I can make out, so did her husband and her parents, the only other people who had heard the clock strike twice.

Then Mary Pollard told another courting story, how a girl told her 'chap' to come early to see her one night, and how he came early and stayed late; and how, next morning, for fear the old folk should hear the double set of footsteps descending the stairs, she carried him down on her back, and how she slipped and fell outside the old folks' door, and the father came out and found the two there.

12

This tale was told with the utmost vigour and gusto, and was received with shouts of laughter. Mary apologised to the 'gentleman' for this tale; giving as an excuse that it was Christmas time.

December 25th. Today, being Christmas Day, I dined at the Gotches'. Present were Mr and Mrs Craft, Whitmore, an American artist, and his wife, young Costa and a Mr Rheam. Afterwards Mr and Mrs Forbes and a Mr Fortescue* and his wife came in.

December 28th. Yesterday afternoon went to Phyllis Gotch's Christmas-tree party at Forbes' studio. Was introduced to Miss Courtney, sister of Leonard Courtney the M.P. She talked about the Cornish dialect, of which she has published a glossary.

Saying: 'As formal as the Mount' (presumably St Michael's Mount), where *formal* means 'old-fashioned'.

December 29th. Last night dined at the Forbes' with the Crafts and Harris.** Passed the Forbes' house again this afternoon, and was shown the house and the baby. Forbes is painting one of the granite carts with its team of four horses.

December 31st. Dined last night at the Crafts' with the Fortescues and a Mr Foster, cousin of the Bolithos. The

*John da Costa (1867–1931), H.M. Rheam (1859–1920) and W.B. Fortescue (1855–1924) were all members of the Newlyn group of artists.
**As was Edwin Harris (1855–1906).

Gotches came in here after dinner, and we had music as usual.

This evening Mrs S. has been telling ghost stories. There is a haunted house in the court behind the Fisherman's Rest. A man one night was sitting there over the fire, brewing some tea, when he heard a creaking in the chamber overhead, as if a heavy person was walking about. He supposed it to be one of the womenfolk, so he shouted up: 'You mind there, what'st doing over stairs? Come down, wilt'st.' 'No come down,' says Mrs S. Then he went to the foot of the stairs and called again – and out of the chamber came a woman in a black silk dress, as it seemed in the darkness, and stood at the top of the landing. 'Who be'st?' he asked. 'Come out of that wilt'st?' But she did not move, so he went into the kitchen, lit a candle, and came out again with it in his hand. There was no one there. He went upstairs and explored the chambers, but found nothing. Then he knew what it was, and rushed out of the house in an agony of terror. But it seems that a ghost, if Cornish, cannot bear the light. Mrs Simons told other eerie tales, of a ghost rattling the *clome* in the *spence* (earthenware in the pantry), and of one driving a solitary householder to climb from her bedroom on to the *ellinhouse* (the slates of a roof).

January 1st, 1893. The New Year opens with what Mrs Simons calls a fine day; that is to say, it is dull, cold, misty, with a drizzling rain now and then, but with little wind. It is the strength of the wind that people here regard most. Last night to supper at the Gotches. We talked about the new poet, Francis Thompson. Mrs Gotch has met him at the

Meynells' and describes him as a thin, shrivelled *atomy* (skeleton). He received a good education but thwarted his father in the choice of a profession, and two years ago he was starving. Dirty scraps of paper used to be thrust into the box of Meynell's magazine *Merry England*. For a long time they stayed there unregarded, but at last Meynell happened to look at one, and was immensely struck with it. They hunted for the poet, and found him selling matches in the Strand, a volume of a Greek poet in one hand and his stock-in-trade in the other. Meynell took him in hand, and has now for two years kept him in food and clothes, receiving poetry in exchange. It is quite the conventional romantic story with the usual sad appendix: now that things are going well with Thompson he is taking to drink.

To shurgie = to act slyly or shyly

A washing tray = a tray or oblong tub used for washing clothes

Saying: 'He lives too near a wood to be frightened by a owl.'

January 5th. Yesterday and today a hard frost, a bitter east wind and some snow. Ten degrees of frost this morning. Such cold weather has not been known here for years. Last night at Miss Courtney's, music and conversation, with a supper. I took a Miss Kendall in to supper, and she read my hand for me, and gave me some surprisingly correct information.

January 6th. Boys everywhere pelting the birds. One of the Newlyn men returned today with four of his fingers frost-bitten. A mist along the coast past Penzance, out of which just the summit of the Mount appeared, like the battlements of an airy castle, cloud-based.

'I'd sooner have a tart than a fuggan,' said the man, 'though it do cost a bit more.' This was when they were discussing the question of beauty versus utility in a wife. A *fuggan* is a lump of dough which working men take out to eat when on a job.

A woman accused of drunkenness says 'I never lift my gown' (i.e. to get at her pocket). 'What she d'ave, she d'ave on the cheap,' Mrs Simons explains.

January 12th. Mrs Simons's grandmother wore a mob cap and a velvet band on her forehead to keep her hair up. She was married to a merchant captain who was captured in the French war, and thrown in a French prison where he remained till the peace. To send him money to keep him alive, she sold all her valuables, silver shoe-buckles, etc., one by one. When everything was gone she took a *cawl* (fish-basket) and went up country (i.e. the Penwith hinterland) selling fish. She would tramp to St Just and back every day; and when she got back, and her children said 'You must be tired, Mother' – 'Tired?' she would say, 'No, fresh as a lark.' There was then a salt-tax from which the fish-buyers and sellers were exempt; and she used to take advantage of this to smuggle salt up country at the bottom of her *cawl*. At last she was caught and sent to prison, where the jailer fell in love with her and wanted to marry her. But her husband at last returned, though he died, mad, in a year.

A saying of hers which Mrs Simons remembers is expressive if not exactly delicate. When annoyed with frivolous chatter, she would get up and go off, saying: 'I'm not fond o' hearing a goose fart.'

January 17th. Dined on Saturday at the Whitmores' with the Crafts and Foster. Foster has 'seen life'. He has been in the backwoods and lived in an Indian camp. Was once offered three squaws by a Sioux chief in exchange for a blanket.

Dined on Sunday with Blackburne. Hall* and Rheam came in, and da Costa. Hall is very quiet and says funny things without the ghost of a smile. Sits with hands folded and pipe in mouth without stirring.

A committee meeting of the 'niggers' (a nigger-minstrels entertainment) at Blackburne's: Rheam, Harris, Craft, Birch.** Birch told of his uncle, who had a glass eye. He used to keep a spare eye with him, in case of accidents. Once his eye-maker made a mistake, and sent a brown eye instead of a blue one. He kept this by him, and one day in the railway train he sat opposite an old lady who saw something remarkable in his appearance and kept staring at his eyes. He objected to this, so waiting till they got to a tunnel he took out his eye in the dark, and put in the brown one. When they got out of the tunnel the dame looked up, and fairly jumped. Now she stared more than ever; so when they got to the next tunnel, he exchanged eyes again. At the next station she fled.

*Fred Hall (1860–1948) a notable member of the colony. As a cartoonist he drew many of his fellow-artists.
**Since Samuel John (Lamorna) Birch has not yet been mentioned (p.16), this must, I think, be Lionel Birch, whose wife wrote a book on Mr and Mrs Forbes.

January 20th. Fine morning. Yesterday afternoon at the Gotches. Went home to dinner with Birch, who is staying at Paul. The old man they call Nimrod, whose name is Tonkin, is a cousin of Mrs Simons. During his wife's lifetime he constructed an elaborate coffin for whichever of them should die first. He spent many evenings over it, decorating it all over with nails arranged as anchors, hearts, etc. When she died she was laid in it, and her best silk dress laid over as a pall. He is a niggardly old fellow, and some say she died of starvation. He used to declare she was as strong as a horse, could eat a whole roasted pilchard at a sitting.

January 21st. Nigger meeting at Blackburne's after tea, and a practice at Gotches after dinner – a very tiring day.
    January month: a Celtic way of saying 'in January'.

January 23rd. Met Cornish, who tells me that some of the older men can count their mackerel using the Cornish numerals. Anything four-legged, he says, brings ill-luck to a boat. It is sufficient to make a chalk drawing of a cat or a dog on a Newlyn boat when building it to make the men pull it to pieces again. To carry a hare's foot or the like on board is very unlucky, and if anything of this kind is found after starting, the men will turn back. As for the Sennen men, who have an incomprehensible stutter in their speech, if when going to the boats they meet a woman, they turn back, and will not go out that day. Small wonder an old Newlyn woman said of fishermen: 'When there's a wind they wussn't go, an' when there's a calm they cussn't go.'

5. Fishermen, Newlyn. 1894

January 29th. The Mousehole men eat their duff before their broth, for when the Spaniards burnt the town the fisher folk were sitting down to dinner – beef and duff. When the Spaniards came, they had just finished their broth, and they had to run, leaving meat and dumplings to the invaders. Ever since they have attacked the duff first.

On Saturday night, the Bramley* supper, which went off very successfully. Speeches by Langley,‡ Forbes, Gotch, etc. Afterwards music.

‡[*Note by Lee*:] This is the first appearance of 'Lamorna'

*Frank Bramley (1857–1915) and Walter Langley (l852–1922) were both established artists.

19

Birch.* I vamped an accompaniment to a comic song by him in broad Lancashire dialect.

Whereas the herring boats like to 'have a board ashore', and so draw up in ranks three or four deep by the quays on first entering, the Plymouth and Dartmouth trawlers come in with nearly all sail set, and drop anchor and bring up flying in mid-harbour. Now they have steam to pull up nets with, they are very much under-manned, three men and a boy being the usual complement for these big boats; whereas the herring smacks, half their size, take six and seven. The boy's place in all weathers is on the gaff.**

February 2nd. The first dose of the entertainment came off last night, and was very successful, especially the comic duet. Tea today with Blackburne – met the Misses De la Condamine, Backhouse and Oldham, the last a remarkably beautiful girl.

At 'Shraff-tide' in Mrs S's youth, the lads and girls used to go down on the rocks and gather 'wrinkles an' lempots' – evidently an old fish-eating Lent custom.

February 6th. If you see a hare, you should tear your shirt or shift, and bad luck will be averted. Meeting a hare when off to market necessitates a return and a fresh start.

Mem: how the Newlyn policeman augments his income; by stalking boys who go out to play *feeps* (pitch and toss).

---

*Lamorna Birch (1869–1955), destined to become one of the best-known members of the group, was a newcomer.
**A spar used in ships to extend the heads of fore-and-aft sails which are not set on stays.

He appears. Money is on the ground – sometimes as much as two or three pounds. 'Whose is this?' No answer so he sweeps it all up and puts it in his pocket.

The night before Frank Runnals died suddenly. Frank's brother, sitting in the kitchen, saw the closed door suddenly open, and after an interval, shut again with a bang. There was no one in the court outside, and no wind. This was a 'token'.

[Here, apart from a welter of small notes, the first volume of the Journal ends. The second volume opens in Cadgwith in March 1897. But there may, of course, be lost volumes.]

1897–1900

Cadgwith, Portloe, London, Mevagissey, Gorran Haven

Cadgwith. March 13th, 1897. Sayings: 'Have you kissed the bullies?' Has your ship touched the shore? (*bullies* = pebbles).

'He went to step in the river and he stanked right in,' said of one who lapses into the vernacular when he is 'cuttin' up'.

To stank is to stamp; *cuttin' up* is talking in a refined way.

Caunce, a pebbled path to a house.

The economics of catching lobsters: A *fleet* of crab-pots for Drew's boat consists of seventy-two pots. Withies cost a shilling for each pot, and making, another shilling. Ropes are necessary, to the amount of three cwt. The total cost of upkeep for a year is £20. A man working all day and an hour in the evening can make two pots. A good average take for a pot is a shilling's worth at each haul. The Drews made £120 last season. Pots are hauled daily if possible; this means two men and a boy to Drews' boat.

The hours of pulling up the pots in the summer vary from one in the morning to midday, according to tide. When they reach midday they go back to one in the morning again.

March 17th. This afternoon the men were teasing the village 'natural', who is deaf and dumb. The rector gave him a boat some time ago. He is very proud of it, and will allow no one to touch it. Last night they had to haul all the boats up, including the natural's, owing to the weather. In doing so, they left a mark of mud on it. Everybody who came along was tackled and led up to the boat, in order to have it explained to them. He did his best to find out who was the culprit. Drew egged him on.

March 20th. In Cornwall, they do not speak of the *lid* of a teapot or saucepan, but of the *cover*. The use of *lid* in this connection for some reason or other, strikes Cornish people as humorous.

The former wrestling champion of Cornwall goes round the district with a greengrocer's cart. He is still the strongest and biggest man in the district, but he has a weak heart and can only do light work. This might be worked up.*

At one o'clock this morning, a vessel laden with granite went ashore in the fog between Coverack and Black Head. The coastguard put out in their boat and saved the crew of fourteen men. The men have indulged in a laughing grumble at the nature of the cargo. No profit for wreckers in a shipload of granite!

Mrs Drew's sister and brother-in-law have been over at Port Isaac, teaching the men and their wives to make and mend nets. It seems incredible, but the people there didn't know how. They used to buy nets, use them till they were falling to pieces, and then buy new ones.

*See Lee's amusing story 'A Strong Man' in *Our Little Town*.

March 23rd. Drews have forty pots out now. All seventy-two are out in summer. Best bottom is sand interspersed with small flat rocks, in about fifty to seventy feet of water.

Sayings: 'He had no tie *up*' where *up* = *on*. Also, in 'no coat *up*, nor no hat *up*, in that bitter cold weather.'

In the summer Dumby, as the deaf-and-dumb 'natural' is called, does not care to light a fire for his tea, but takes the tea-pot out and begs some hot water. Once the boys began to throw stones at the tea-pot. Dumby thought they were aiming at him; he put the tea-pot down and searched for stones to throw back. Whilst his back was turned, a well-aimed stone smashed the tea-pot to atoms. Of course, Dumby didn't hear the smash, and continued to battle all unconscious. Having routed his enemies, he turned to pick the tea-pot up. Then his rage was terrific. Yet he is the best maker of store-pots in the village. Slow, but very careful and conscientious.

When his friends became outrageous he used to run up to his friend the rector, who was also a JP, and apply for a summons. The rector would pretend to take down the names and Dumby would depart content. But as he grows older he is getting more irritable, or *taissy*, as they say here. He is now a bugbear for local toddlers. I heard a little girl quieting her squalling charge with 'Dumby'll get you.'

More vocabulary:

Cuffas at Cadgwith and Coverack = *poochas* elsewhere in Cornwall = 'she-crabs' – small crabs fetching three-half-pence each.

A *preen* is a foot-long stick of hazel or blackthorn or a 'furzy-stick' with a kind of barb near the thick end – used to fasten down the bait in a pot. Three preens to each pot.

[Clearly, Lee moved to London at this point, and there are many London jottings. His next Cornish entry is from Portloe, in September 1898, eighteen months later.]

Portloe. September, 1898. About fifty boats at Portloe, one to each man; but as they mostly go out two in a boat, half the boats are usually laid up.

> Spark and Beauty,
> Neat and Comely,
> Brisk and Lively.

These are names of oxen used for ploughing. Oxen still plough at a farm near Mevagissey.

Perhaps it is the old spirit of enterprise that made pirates of Cornishmen formerly, which now leads them to fish in each other's waters. Thus Gorran men fish off Portloe and Mevagissey, Mevagissey men off Gorran, Portloe men off Gorran and Falmouth, and so on.

Had a chat with the coastguard chief officer this morning. An admirable man, universally liked and respected. Even my caustic neighbour, J. Gribble, scoffs not at him. He has made Portloe the soberest and best-conducted station on the coast; and before his time it was a byword. 'Mind, if you go to the public house, you'll find me there,' he says.

The coastguard is a strong believer in tobacco, but always comes out of doors to smoke, as the missus doesn't like the smell. J. Gribble, hearing this, said that if *his* missus felt that way, 'twould be: 'Step outside for a minute, will 'ee, missus: I want to smokie.'

6. Portloe, 1911

They say in Portloe that 'sharks make good bait – they smill that wild; terrible wild sharks do smill'.

A plague of caterpillars infests the place. Having reduced the cabbages to forlorn wrecks, they are invading the coastguard station in force, and a naval demonstration is projected against them.

Fisherman takes a short broken-stemmed black clay from his pocket, pulls down his guernsey, extracts a loose match from the bottom fold thereof, and lights up.

Saying: 'If you want clear water, you must go to the head of the well', i.e. no use dealing with subordinates.

Of custards: 'We spin them up with a' aig, and then bake them'.

Names: Cornelius, pronounced Cornaylius. His wife calls him Cornell; the village calls him Naylie.

The great worry of the coastguard chief is the disinclination of his men to walk the cliffs by night without a lantern, lanterns being forbidden by the regulations. One young fellow has lately gone out of his mind, through seeing a ghost up 'Craze' (Caerhays) way.

When there is a wreck, two coastguardsmen stand one on each side of the path on the cliff, and all the 'salvers' have to pass between them. Nothing may be kept, unless it is the property of one of the crew and has been presented to the salver by the owner.

John Gribble's father has been weaving stars and frames of wheat, oats and barley for the harvest festival at the Wesleyan Chapel. He has made seventy of these, and is very proud of them.

Saying: 'A proper blind man: one properly blind', i.e. completely blind.

Salting pilchards: a girl scraping the salt in a snowy heap; a man rubbing the salt inside the fish; a woman packing them in an earthenware pan; a tribe of pretty children sitting cross-legged around, looking on.

Saying: 'We hailed them and didn't get a *mouth-speech* out of them' (cf. eyesight).

As the old man said up to the land-and-sea thanksgiving, when he strung three dried pilchards over the chapel door: 'The Lord loveth a cheerful giver, and if I guv more I'd be apt to grumble.'

September 15th. Last night down on the beach to see the pilchards. Seven boats came in with from 1,500 down. Easterly wind so first of all they had to be hauled up: a picturesque enough sight. Under a moonless, starry sky, the beach was alive with white jackets. Three or four lanterns floating about mysteriously. The boats were heavy. Round each as it was hauled up were gathered fourteen or fifteen men. One at the stern held a rope in one hand, and clutched his lantern to his breast with the other, for him to guide the boat over the 'ways' (timber rollers laid at intervals before it). The lantern caught here a face, here an elbow, here a trunk, rarely a pair of legs; enviously distorting the figures, making hunchbacks, cripples, miracles of ugliness of the straightest and comeliest. One boat hauled up, a search with lanterns for the 'ways', which were then set for the next. Lanterns set on the beach here and there to light the course. 'Haul – up with her! Haul – up with her!', at regular intervals: all the white jackets swaying forward together; till they made a great effort and ran the boat right up.

When all the boats were up, the pilchards were taken out. Two men, one on each side of the boat, manipulated the net, in which the fish came now singly, now in patches. Some skill is required in getting the fish out. John J. pushed one youngster aside and showed him the way: a combined tug and double shake, and the gills are disentangled and the fish falls with a slap in the well of the boat. A clumsy hand will pull the body off and leave the head.

A lantern fixed to a pole gives light. A fresh sweet sea-smell, slightly tainted with paraffin from the lamp below. Some men were throwing the fish from the boats into the *gurries* or hand-barrows. Much shouting to and fro. The fish gleamed silver with here and there a red, opaline spark. They were stiff to the hand; slightly curved one way or another. Their large, pearly scales came off on everything. Cats were wandering about the beach, seeking what they might devour. Behind, up the cove, square lighted windows. Below, the sea grumbling at the robbers. Men approached one another, peering, with a tentative 'Hullo! That you, Johnny?' 'Iss: Jacky, b'lieve?'*

September 17th. Butter made here by hand from scalded cream. Churns unknown. In furnishing a house, the married couple aim at 'a dresser full o' cloam'. This is, or was, half the battle. A grandfather clock was the first luxury. It might be a brass-faced one or what is called in Portloe 'a flowery-faced wan'.

---

*This incident is worked up into a passage in *Cynthia in the West*, chapter 10.

The hill over cove to the right, in Portloe, is called 'Jacka'. The hill beyond is 'the Downs'.

Maxims are games with marbles, coins and the like to pass the time away. Also, more generally, tricks.

'When the mackerel begin to *schoolie*': go in shoals.

Among his other functions, J. Gribble is assistant layer-out and undertaker to the district. The people here have an invincible repugnance to touching a corpse. But J.G. says: 'Man couldn't hurt me when alive, so idn' goin' to hurt me when e's dead.' Called up from the beach by a boy, not knowing for what, he finds it is a corpse; he must take tar off hands before touching. One old man swelled 'tremenjous' after being measured for his coffin. 'Put cover on,' says J.G. 'I'll push 'un down.' He does so with his knees as for a portmanteau. 'Now old bloke's all snug.' says J.G.

September 28th. Saying: 'There was some round wans going up there, I can tell 'ee,' i.e. some hard swearing.

When one loses one's way, one should turn one's glove inside out.

Gorran coastguard's tale: the water tanks in Gorran are small, and the competition for washing-water so keen on Mondays, that when Mr Moyse was there he used to come upon men stealthily pumping at twelve o'clock on Sunday night, one hand on the pump to keep it from creaking. Clothes on the line sometimes by four a.m.

John (Gribble) thinks James (Johns) is foolish to spend so much money on his house. It is only a lease-hold property, dependent on two lives, and lives are 'oncertain'.

'Soon' you see' crab you want 'm'. Notice the economy of speech.

October 1st. 'The hen stole her nest' – went and sat out in the bushes.

Cluck = broody.

The old builder who died today left £12,000. He would have left more, but used to give away money right and left when drunk. He was subject to fits; but ask him the time sharply when they were coming on, and they wouldn't come. Died, says J.G., from drinking furniture polish. Courted a woman thirty years and then jilted her. By all accounts, he wanted to marry young, but the maid said, 'Wait till you've got on a bit.' He got on a bit. The maid said, 'Wait till you've got on a bit more.' He got on a bit more. Then he got on a lot more; too much, and she wud'n good enough.

Top hats are called 'drums' or 'drum hats' here. Uncle Willy is the only one who is allowed to wear the headgear without criticism. Another man coming to chapel in one today, elicited sarcasm from J.G.: 'Drum beatin'; we shall have a gale o' wind tomorrow.' 'That 'at was cast in a mould when Adam weared slippers.' Most of the older men wear soft black wideawakes, and a neckerchief. The younger men wear bowlers and white collars.

The seat on Jacka is an old spar supported by heaps of stones. This is Uncle Willy's seat, and he sits in the sun, his stick behind him (no handle; he holds it fine-lady fashion) sucking away at his pipe, his tongue ready with a retort or a yarn. Someone gives him a match and bids him be off into the *lew* and light his pipe again. Off he goes, and comes back puffing. It seems to me, it is the chief occupation and aim in life of every person and thing in Cornwall, this 'getting into the lew'.

Notice the attitudes of a group of talkers. Some leaning over the side of a boat, intently staring at her bottom. Another standing with his back to everybody else, gazing up town. Others, sitting on timber or ground. Nobody looking at anybody else. The result when they are talking to a stranger who does not know the voices is a curious ventriloquial effect. All the voices seem to come from one person – which person one can't tell.

October 7th. Yesterday found J.G. occupied in 'laying-in' the *caunce* (yard, paved surface before a dwelling-house). He was fixing afresh some of the stones at the edge which had got loose. The bed-rock being just beneath, he experienced some trouble. While working, he cynicised on women, his wife standing by with a sad, tolerant smile on her lips. Woman's one aim was to catch her man. When he's caught, he's a mouse in a trap, or a criminal at the treadmill.

A dog in the village was bitten or stung by an adder, it is supposed. The dog's master went to St Austell (twelve miles) yesterday to see a certain man there and get him to charm the dog. Faith is necessary. A woman was stung; the charmer took her hand, blew on it, and asked 'Have 'ee faith in the charm?' 'No, I don't think so,' said she. He refused to proceed.

'The spirit of the devil's in their stummicks'. This remark of J.G.'s was occasioned by the sight of his friend Williams coming across to chapel with an armful of ivy. The church had ivy; so must they. This spirit of emulation is most unchristian in J.G.'s opinion. He is also wroth at their having the auction of produce immediately after the service. The Book says the money-lenders were driven out of the temple.

J.G. says that his neighbour James Johns, constantly re-painting his house, is 'like Gaygle with his ropes of sand'. Gaygle = Tregeagle.*

October 8th. An auction sale. Mrs Dawe buying useless rubbish; her husband hovering behind the crowd, shouting unregarded warnings to her: 'Now Sarann, what do 'ee want with half-a-hundredweight o' lead pipin'? I ask 'ee, what do 'ee want wid'n?' Old hens are for sale: 'What do 'ee want with a old hen – take six weeks to bile and a fortnight to eat – that's eight weeks!' The piano was bought for 5/6. There was keen competition for feather 'tyes' (mattresses) sold by the pound. New goose-feathers are worth a shilling a lb. Old desks and secretaires are bought on spec by the villagers. There may be secret drawers in them, which may contain valuables. Saying: 'Turn the best side towards London.'

William the shoemaker has a hard time of it in the winter. J.G. has counted as many as four and twenty able-bodied fishermen in his shop, which is no bigger than a

---

*Tregeagle, who flourished in the Cromwellian period, was an unjust and cruel bailiff of the lords of Lanhydrock, and he has had grafted onto him several legends perhaps formerly attributed to the devil. His uneasy spirit is doomed to spin ropes of sand, and to drain Dozmary Pool with a leaky limpet-shell.

hat-box. Sometimes the chaff and practical jokes are more than he can bear; he weeps and declares he'll give up the shop. When he goes out for a moment, they stick a bit of wax to his seat, etc. J.G. he regards as the ringleader or 'king', as they say here. The men in that little shop stand shoulder to shoulder. The shop is littered with scraps of leather; the window is broken, patched, never cleaned; yet he knows everybody that passes, and though living in this underground den, he is the man to get information from. No minutest feather of gossip flies up the street without blowing into his door. The door, by the way, and the step or so within, are dignified by the name of 'the lobby': 'Plenty of room in the lobby.'*

Male ablutions, when of more than a perfunctory kind, are conducted in the front garden. There is no professional barber in Portloe. If you want to get shaved and don't care to do it yourself, you stand at your door with razor, towel, basin and soap, etc., until a friendly mortal passes. Him you enlist, and bring a chair into the yard or garden, and sit and submit to his tender mercies. It is not etiquette to offer payment, but if a small boy or girl of the tonsor's begetting is around, you offer the child a penny for sweets.

Outside his house J.G. had a myrtle of which he was proud, tending it carefully. A woman-neighbour, jealous of the fine plant, threw boiling water over it, but did not succeed in killing it.

James Johns coming back from Treganna, Mrs J. inquires for news. None. Has he seen anybody in the street? Nobody to speak of. Well, she never knew such a man. But

*See *Our Little Town*, chapter I.

further inquiries elicit the fact that he has seen a girl doing something at the bedroom window of a certain farm house. Mrs J. at once starts speculating. That was Jim's room and hasn't been papered since he went to America thirty years ago. No, says J. it wasn't that room. Was it the end room? No, the middle one. Ah! the window blind of the middle room got out of order last winter. The maid was surely mending it. And Mrs J. is happy.

An old farmer hereabouts went to a St Austell bank to cash a draft. They gave him notes. He was met on his return by his housekeeper, who managed his affairs: 'Why, maister, what 'ave 'ee got there? You know we 'aven't got nowhere in the 'ous to put notes, except where the mice can get at 'em. Go thee'st back and get gold for 'em.' And back he went. It was said of this old farmer that he turned his money in his pocket so often, that it was too thin to pass for currency.

October 13th. Jimmy the Fiddler lives alone. His father was Jimmy the Fiddler before him. He loves to get a crowd of small children in his cottage and play to them. They sit as quiet as mice. Ruddy face, white hair and whiskers, upper lip clean shaven. Trots down to beach when fish is coming in, and someone generally gives him half a hundred of pilchards (which he is accused of selling), or a couple of small ray, the only fish he has a relish for. Handy man – makes picture frames. If he takes payment his club-pension is in danger.

This afternoon, back to William, the shoemaker's shop (William Rundle). His hands are busy all the time; when he wants another tool, he makes a bird-like dive, without

7. Fishermen at Portloe, 1912

looking, and fetches it up. Sheets of leather in the corner behind, hammers and boards on the ground to the right, wax ends on the shelf to the right, in front, on the table, nails, *taps*, awls, scraps of leather, lasts on the table to the left in front, water for soaking leather underneath to the left, and at his left-hand a lap-stone for hammering on. However busy he may be, his slanting eyes go up when he hears wheels or footsteps; he peers through the window, moving his head this way and that, and the passer is registered. When he gets teased, he picks up his hammer. Why do they interfere with him? He flourishes the hammer and invites one and all to show their pluck by letting him hit their hands. 'That's the only answer William have got,' was explained to me.

The talk at William's turned to wrecking. Some

puncheons of spirits have been picked up off Land's End. What is a puncheon? Naylie, the authority on spirituous matters was appealed to, and delivered the dictum that a puncheon is the biggest kind of barrel that *is* a barrel. The liquor one gets from wrecks is of marvellous quality; the rum, for example, white as milk. Naylie knew of instances when men have got drunk from breathing over the bung-hole of a wrecked cask. A queer race with coastguardsmen was told of. A keg of rum, some wreckers on the shore. Coastguardsmen on the cliff, hurrying down. 'Fill your bellies, men.' They drink and drink. One rolls over. The coastguardsmen are nearing. Another of the drinkers falls over, and another. The coastguards are at hand. The one hero not prostrate collects his strength, and staves in the barrel.

It is unlucky to read the marriage service before you have gone through the ceremony. Mrs Johns got her sister to read it through several times to her.

A spar in the cove. Coastguardsmen and I watched it: 'How many eyes on that spar, d'ye think?' said the coastguard. Not a soul visible on the beach. It came nearer and nearer and suddenly there were men with lines and grapnels on the rocks on either side, and a swarm of young and old on the beach. One old man was pointed out to me in particular as an inveterate wrecker. If there was a chance of obtaining that spar by getting wet through, wet through he would get.

October 14th. More wrecking this afternoon. Three young men risked their lives for a plank, some bits of board, and an empty barrel.

October 15th. Onions! Tons of them washed ashore on all the beaches. Every sack, bag, washing-tray and basket in Portloe full of them. Rows of them drying on walls and window-sills; and thousands still strewn on the shore, piled up between the rocks, wedged into every corner, floating in patches and wreaths in the water in the cove and outside. Presumably from a Jersey vessel, run into and sunk the day before yesterday. J.G. enticed me down to the beach and made me help fill a basket. When we came up he sat on the wall and chuckled till the tears came: 'Mr Lee's been wreckin'. 'E's branded. 'E's a Cornish wrecker sure 'nough. Somethin' to tell 'es people when 'e go 'ome.'

Padstow men don't *coincide* with strangers, and aren't sociable.

A man at Trewartha got drunk and *scat up* the *cloam*. So next day his wife 'gave him a sherdy pasty for *crowst*,'* (a pasty made with fragments of earthenware).

Old Mrs G. thinks Providence is directly responsible for sending onions instead of oranges. If it had been oranges, all the children, and a good many of the grown-ups, would have been terribly ill by now. But the Breton onion-sellers who come selling onions 'very sheap' will do badly in Portloe this year.

Went to J.G.'s this afternoon. A charwoman in. J.G. told me about her afterwards. She was house-keeper at a farm and had a very comfortable berth, but the 'sherdy-pasty man' [see above] came along, a sorrowing widower, and persuaded her to marry him. He ate too plenteously of the wedding feast, had to call in the doctor next day, was

*Elevenses

very ill, and went on the parish as soon as he recovered, so she has to go out charring. I saw the man, limping across a field.

The coastguard men are not above doing a little on their own account in the wrecking. J.G. saw three of them this morning with bundles on their backs, *not* bound for the watch-house. Two men who were here lately used to steal the rabbits out of J.G.'s gins. He caught them both in the act.

Local wrath at the pride of the modern farmer. In the old days the wealthiest folk were Jacky this and Tommy that; now, if a man farms three acres and owes more than he has ever owned, you must 'Mister' him when he deigns to notice you.

When the neck was cried,* neck-cakes were baked; round flat cakes six inches across. These were distributed to all assisting, and sent round to acquaintances.

J.G. to his mother, who is keeping me back while she gossips: 'Shall I lend 'ee a pair o' scissors, mother, to cut that yarn?'

When the fishing fleet is out in the Channel, there is always a Dutch *couper* about, with a supply of baccy and liquor. The French boats will always give a supply of weak brandy to those who ask, or will fill a bottle with better stuff for a few pence. It is fun to hear their *pallyvoozing*.

October 18th. Sam Peter slouching off, gun over shoulder.

---

*'To cry the neck' is to shout around the corn-field in celebration of the neck, the last armful of corn cut. The neck is often twisted into a miniature sheaf.

It is an old army Snider that has been turned into a breechloader.

Portloe wreck mad. A big four-master on the Manacles. 160 missing out of 200. Will any of the wreckage come this way? All the village in oilskins on Jacks, watching the sea and Portloe. A barrel of brandy picked up at Portholland yesterday by two men. Hence, says J.G., handed over to the coastguards, because 'You must be alone if you want to do a roguery'. Two men swear to a secret, but 'fore long, one mouth spits in another, and another in another.' For every scrap of wreckage that comes ashore and into the hands of the coastguard, two forms have to be signed, with full description, where and when picked up, state of tide, whether floating, bumping or ashore, marks, owner's name if known, and other particulars. Eight hatches have been picked up, an eighteen foot plank, a sheep, which has to be buried by the coastguard, and will cost the country four shillings; and any amount of miscellaneous stuff. And, says Mr Moyes the coastguard, 'Every iotum' must be accounted for.

James Johns is making a garden. Lots of people have promised him flowers but he doesn't set much store by promises. He knows the people who, when they are asked to do a thing, say 'Ess-ess-ess-ess'. He doesn't believe in 'Ess-ess' people. When a man says 'Well, I'll see what I can do,' or 'Don't know, but I'll try,' then he has confidence in him. The 'I'll try' man for him; not the 'Ess-ess-ess-ess' man.

October 19th. Naylie, christened Cornelius, told me that in his youth a farm labourer's wages were seven shillings a week. The daily fare was pilchards and potatoes; on Sundays a slice of fat pork, about four inches square and an inch thick, was baked in the middle of a potato pie. A common article of diet was the bannock, an immense flat cake of barley-bread, baked on a hot iron plate. Many's the time Naylie has slipped into the kitchen when his mother's back was turned, torn off the corner of the half-baked bannock, dipped it in the treacle-jar, and devoured it. Note the treacle; sugar was too dear; so was tea. A substitute for tea was a crust burnt brown and soaked in hot water. There was no such thing as matches in Portloe in those days. Portloe eats more meat in a week now than it did in years in the old days.

Clane turnip pasty, i.e. meat and turnips, with no admixture of potatoes.

Great catch of plaice last night: forty score between five boats. One boat had twelve and a half score, an unprecedented number. Eight score is considered good.

October 22nd. Sayings: 'He's neither upright nor down straight'.

> 'Saturday's moon, the sailor's doom
> Come once in seven year, come once too soon.'

'What are 'ee doin'?' 'Helpin' Uncle Antony to kill dead mice' – i.e. nothing.'

'James is 'carty', i.e. a hearty eater.

October 24th. Portloe has gone *spillerin'* this morning: four in a boat. Went down beach after breakfast and saw them baiting the hooks. Three men baiting, and one cutting up cuttle. The *spiller-crave* was stuck upright in a cleft or between the bars of a crab-pot. *Spiller*, as baited, coiled in a box, the hooks with their grey-black bait on, all on one side of the box. To each *spiller* 300 hooks, to each box three *spillers*. Bait cut up on a little board. Fragments of cuttle, iridescent with blues and pinks, lying about. Men's hands a rich black, especially inner side of fingers. A curious odour of mingled fish and chemicals, but this may have been the rotten onions of ten days ago.*

Last time Naylie got drunk was when the Band of Hope came here. He always gets drunk then on principle, to show he isn't one of them. At seventy, and 'on the parish', Naylie expresses a wish that he could begin again at seventeen, living all his life over again as it has been, drunks and all.

November 19th. London, at the Cornish Association. A lecture by Silas Hocking. Introduced to him, and to Canon Shuttleworth. The latter told me of a man whose banns were put up in his parish. After the first asking the man came to him: 'Mr S., those banns, I've something to ask 'ee. Those banns, can I have 'em changed? I've been a-thinkin', and I'd rather 'ave 'er sister.' 'Of course,' said Mr S. 'you can marry whom you please; but the banns will have to be put up again.' 'But, Mr S, will that be another

---

*According to Morton Nance, in *A Glossary of Cornish Sea-words*, a *spiller* is 'a tackle, smaller than a *boulter*, used for smaller fish.' The *boulter* is a longer line. The *crave* is a cleft stick upon which a *spiller* is arranged, as Lee says. According to Nance, it seems to be a Portloe variant of the commoner form *claves*.

half-crown for me to pay?' 'Of course.' 'H'm. Mr S., I think I'll leave 'en as 'tes.'

Silas Hocking told of the old woman who bemoaned the increase of infidelity. They denied a 'personal devil' now, they denied hell and eternal torment. Soon, she said, there'd be no comfort left in religion at all.

[*March 1900* finds Lee at Mevagissey, staying with a Mr and Mrs Way. He is surprised to find that Mevagissey is lit with electric light!]*

Fishermen on jetty, chaffing one another on their appetites. One: 'Well, I'd rather ait my wife's pincushions stuffed full o' pins than that bit o' conger.'

J. Way says that fishing is not hard work, except the hour or so of net-pulling. Ashore, the owners of boats and nets work, the single-share men stand about and gossip, and muddle their heads with interminable arguments.

Today, the nets going aboard, ready for mackerel driving. Carts on the jetty, other nets descending from upper windows. About forty men, perhaps, at work, while several hundred stand and look on, in groups on the jetty, lined against walls, leaning out of windows. No working man has so much idle time as the fisherman.

Many here are too lazy to use their 'apparatus' (cooking stoves). They send everything to be cooked to the communal bakehouse. Charge, for a large dinner, meat, potatoes, and perhaps some pastry on top, a penny; for small dishes a halfpenny. Mrs Way disapproves. The food tastes of everything else in the oven, and often it is burnt

*Mevagissey was the first town in Cornwall to be lit by electric light, in 1896.

8. Mevagissey, Inner Harbour, 1909

tastes of everything else in the oven, and often it is burnt into the bargain.

Mrs Way tells of the coming of the cholera* to Cornwall; how a fisherman here saw a box floating, and picked it up, and brought it ashore and examined it, and found it full of clothes. When he dipped the clothes in the sea to wash them, a 'gashly white froth' ascended from them. He died in a few hours. In a few days the disease had firm hold. Some fled to other towns, others put up tents on the cliffs. One lady left, stayed away six months, returned and was dead in a week. The dead were buried in a special corner of the church-yard. The grass grows rank and strangely green.

More of the cholera. How the 'resurrection men' went about with a tarry sheet, into which the dead, and presumably dead, were heaved and hurried off. Martin Dunn (an old man Lee met) grew weary of exile from Mevagissey, and returned, (being then young and strong) to find the town empty, the houses locked, and all the living camped out on the cliff. Dunn himself took possession of a cow-house, stopping with straw all the openings through which the townward wind could penetrate. One talked to a man at one's door, one parted from him, went for a stroll, and returned to find that he was dead *and buried*.

Sayings:

Up a man, getting on for manhood

fightable, fighting mad

'A good little maid, but then she've *no age in her* – just on twelve.'

---

*A severe outbreak of cholera occurred in Mevagissey in 1849. See Charles Kingsley's novel *Two Years Ago*.

'The maid said to 'en, you'm a lazy, taissy man, and he didn' *take it up*' i.e. deny it or answer back.

Tom, a Breage man, stands at the corner with a policeman and criticises the maids. One has to be very careful here. Pass the time of day with a maid once, and tongues clack. Twice, you're hooked.

Mem. Mevagissey after a storm in the old days of thatched roofs; streets strewn with straw 'like a farm-yard', and the thatchers going up and down with their ladders. Note the expression 'hollen like a thatcher' from the distance their voice must carry.

Woman in Mevagissey *streaming* an upstairs window by lowering the upper sash a little way and pouring cupfuls of water between upper and under.

Gorran Haven, April 2nd. A typical gathering in the 'Town Hall' (a disused lime-kiln); lounging against the wall, hands in pockets, bodies twisted. Now and then a hand snatched from a pocket to emphasise a point. Topics: sea-boots, whether possible to keep legs dry with them, whatever their length. Decided in negative. Comparative merits of various boats. Was the defeat of the new boat in a recent regatta attributable to the centre keel, or to her newness or to her new sails? Was the *Dodo* too broad across the hatches? Did So and So pass a certain point to windward or to leeward of Such and Such? The size of certain sails and their merits – 'Like a board', etc. Portloe and Portscatho men refuse to race Gorran men. They are barred from competing in regattas. There is a theory that a white sail means the boat is in debt. A white sail with a brown patch means 'The patch is paid for; I'm owing for the rest.'

After tea, the 'Town Hall' is given over to marbles. 'Don't allow ut when we'm reading the papers.'

Sayings: 'A black easterly – the worst wind that do blaw.' Hence, presumably 'Easterly wind stew' – potatoes, etc., well seasoned, but without meat or fish.

'Pay 'ee Saturday'. 'Saturday never come in this place.'

1903

Mawgan-in-Pydar (St Mawgan)

[Now comes what in my view is the most interesting part of the Journal, the residence in Mawgan-in-Pydar, in inland Cornwall, but not far from Newquay. By 1903, when he went there, Lee was a very accomplished writer.]

January 4th, 1903. The yarn told by Henry at the tea, of the man who used to wear a box hat on such occasions, and set it mouth upwards on his knees, and swept now a cake, now a bun into the receptacle, and somehow got the full hat on his head when he rose to go!

Old John James's account of Mawgan Choir in the old days, when the music was supplied by two flutes, two clarinets, and a bass viol; who, when Parson announced 'Let us sing . . . etc.' sounded in succession the notes of the common chord, from top to bottom; not as in Dolton (in Devon) from bottom to top. And how, on one occasion, when the musicians were not there (and usually, in that case, the parson would omit the invitation to sing, but the gallery was dark, and he near-sighted, and he made a mistake), the only minstrels present being Landlord Gilbert and three or four boys, G. rose to the occasion, stood up,

48

9. The Parish Church, St Mawgan-in-Pydar, *c.* 1890

and chanted the notes of the common chord from top to bottom, as if they were playing instruments.

Philip's yarn last night of one who tealed ten yards of roasted potatoes. The tubers had been planted in a bit of ground partially reclaimed from the moor, but not properly cleared of furze roots. The furze was set afire, and the fire spread underground. Result as above.

Yarn in Park Eglos of a notable drinker, one who after nineteen half pints, apologised to his landlady for departing, saying that he was not in the best of health, but would come again and drink to better purpose of her excellent ale. It was he into whose quart pot somebody dropped a dead mouse. After swigging he began to cough: 'What's the matter?' 'Awnly a bit of hop got in my droat.'

Of Philip's Rose, a perfect retriever: would carry a rabbit half a mile; till one day, P. being overladen, bade her carry the rabbit all the way home. She did, but never retrieved again.

Christmas visit from St Columb handbell ringers. Four, each with two bells. Handles of bells set at an angle. They stood in a semi-circle, their music (printed in figures) on the table before them. Bells rung with a sway of the body, arms swinging up to head level. Tunes and chimes. In ringing changes, the ringers shifted places, so that the bells were always rung in the same order from right to left. Solemn faces. Three imbibed beer; the fourth was a 'teetotaller' and took port wine, with hot water and sugar.

For thirty years in succession, says John James, the carol 'Awake, Awake' was sung on Christmas Day in Mawgan church. He it was who taught the present party to sing it. The attitudes are characteristic. Willy Charles, leader, hands in pocket, eyes shut, head thrown back. Nick Lobb, ditto, his head still further back, and eyes on ceiling. Young Sam gazes at the ground. John Walters leaning against a door-post.

Traditional way of singing carols: one of the Watergate party said: 'We sing it ('Awake') different from Mawgan, and Mawgan again sing it different from Lower St Columb, and that's where 'tis.'

Mrs Davie: 'That's a good old carol, Mr Hawken.'

Bill Hawken: 'Iss; you can't wear 'en out.'

The present squire loves trees.* A tree in the churchyard was threatening to bring down the wall. It was proposed to cut it down. 'No', said squire, 'if the wall falls I can and will repair it in a week; but the tree once fallen . . . ' However, advantage was taken of his absence in London, and the tree was felled.

*See the story 'Langarrock Great Tree', in *Our Little Town*.

January 5th. Gilbert senior was very poor when he married. His wife's parents disapproved of the match, and refused to assist the young couple. There was a great wrestling match at Truro, the first prize being five pounds. He determined to try for it, though he had never taken part in any but small local matches. So he started off early in the morning, carrying with him some rashers of bacon, all he could afford for his breakfast. He walked to Ladock, where he called at a cottage and asked the old woman to fry his bacon. The sleepy careless dame contrived to tip the frying-pan into the fire. On went G. to walk the rest of the twenty miles breakfastless. The tale ends happily – he threw the champion and returned with the £5, which meant so much for him, in his pocket.

Reuben Rosevear tells how in the old days, whenever any striking, especially farcical, incident occurred, one or two would get together and concoct a rude 'ballet' thereon – e.g. of the adventures of the young men and the three maidens returning home from St Columb, when one of the latter was 'taken bad' with wind in the stomach, and Reuben and another unlaced her and dosed her with peppermint bullseyes. The event was celebrated in 'bridle verse' – not over-refined, but vigorous enough, no doubt.

Wrestling matches at Mawgan used to extend over several days. The first was given over to the boys, who were as keen about it as the men. Each village had its juvenile champion, and each would send its representatives.

January 7th. Bill Hawken and the badger: 'I've got 'en!' Pause. 'And he's got me! Ow! (to the badger) You leave go of me, and I'll leave go of you!'

Eplett's description of a paltry wayside ale-house: 'Tied to the hedge by a bramble'.

W.W. tells of the great annual sing-song of Dolton (in Devon) in his young days. It was the day when everybody paid his shoe-maker's bill. The old cobbler hired a room at the inn and invited all his customers. His wife, who had book-learning, sat in a side room, receiving and receipting, and at the table sat the company, passing round the ale, and singing their songs in turn.

W.W. remembers the appearance in Dolton of an ex-prisoner of the Turks – tongueless and with scalloped ears. He did not beg but, arrived at the first paved front yard, knelt and began to weed it. Awe amongst the small boys.

W.W. notes as peculiar the custom of tolling first on the tenor, and then for the last minute on the upper bell.

Jacky Kent returning from the inn, wanders into a ploughed field, and begins abusing the authorities: 'They didn't ought to plough the roads'.

Jacky, somewhat overcome with liquor, essays to sing carols, but cannot keep off the track of Old Dog Tray:

> Thus: 'Put on thy strength, O Jerusalem;
>   He's gentle and he's kind,
>   His tail hangs down behind.'

Miss Houghton keeps shop in a haphazard way.* Her hours are the latest in Mawgan – seldom in bed before midnight, and at nine the schoolchildren are kicking at the door, trying to rouse her from her beauty-sleep. The shop,

*See the story 'The White Bonnet', in *Our Little Town*.

the parlour, the stairs are crowded with goods in admired disorder. Miss G. goes to purchase shoes. One is found to fit her, but the fellow has disappeared, found two days after in an attic. Shop only holds one customer at a time. The others must wait in the garden.

January 9th. 'I'm so weak as a robin,' says Aunt. Why a robin? – stout-hearted, pugnacious bird!

January 10th. Since the land at Winsor is such good land, how is it that Hortop failed to make it pay? Daily papers, says Reuben Rosevear. Hortop's case is no uncommon one hereabouts. He is afflicted with *cacoethes legendi*.* Instead of attending to his business in the morning, he comes down to the post office, waits until the post comes in, seizes his *Western Morning News*, and wastes a couple of hours wading through it. All very well, says R., if you wait till the evening; but to read a morning paper in the morning spells ruin in a farmer. Another case of a young farmer up St Columb way, whose farm is on the main road. At harvest time he would be by the gate, would waylay the postman, call his men from their work, and sit down to read the news aloud to them. Consequence: half the crop remained uncarried and had spoilt. 'If he choose to pay me for hearing 'en read, 'tis no affair of mine,' said one.

Grandfer Charles played the bass viol in Mawgan church when he was yet too small to carry it there without assistance. He and the Pascoes, clarinettists, father and son, used to attend Mass with their instruments, and when the

*A mania for reading.

R.C. service was over, would go across to the church and take their places in the gallery.

January 12th. John Eplett and Reuben Rosevear on the old smuggling days. The men of Mawgan parish seldom initiated a venture. The 'venturers' were generally from St Austell way: men of Roche or St Dennis. Trevarrian and Tregurrian men acted as guides. Eplett tells of one affray at Beacon Cove, where the preventive men were literally whipped off by the men of St Dennis, who leapt off their ponies and donkeys and lashed the officers with their heavy thongs till they fled howling.

A cave in Beacon Cove was a favourite hiding-place for a *kag*. A farmer had a cask 'run' for him. Two, one Fradd and another, took the keg up from the cave to the farm. 'Let's taste 'un first,' said the farmer. The keg was tapped and a jugful of neat brandy poured out. The farmer swigged. All right. 'Jane, go overstairs and fetch the three pound.' Jane went, taking the candle with her. Fradd felt for the jug in the dark, drank, and passed it to his companion. Thrice it went to and fro before the maid returned. And then: 'Well, we managed to steer to the door all right, but I reckon both of us fell down twenty times going up the hill. Terrible strong stuff.'

Is there still any smuggling going on? Well, Mr Glanville, Lord Falmouth's head steward, told Eplett the following incident the other day when they were out shooting at Carnanton. In the course of his duty he had to make the round of a number of deserted mine-shafts, and estimate the cost of filling them in. He inspected two or three, and his calculations of their probable depth passed unchallenged by the men who were guiding him. Then he came to another, and looked in. 'Hm, about so many feet deep.' 'No, tidn' so deep as that, mister.' 'Oh, how do you know? Lost a cow down it?' 'No, mister, never lost no cow.' 'A horse, then?' 'No, nor yet a horse.' 'Then it must have been a goat, or else a donkey.' 'Well, to tell 'ee the truth, you'm wrong again.' 'Come, tell me.' 'Aw, couldn' tell 'ee how I do knaw, but I reckon I do knaw how long a rope it take to get to the bottom of that shaft, and I won't say no more.'

Lillington (gamekeeper) and the coastguard chaffing each other. Says coastguard: 'I reckon you've come down to see I don't do no poaching; and I've got an eye 'pon you to see you don't do no wrecking.'

Of the Mawgan band, which fell in pieces chiefly for the lack of a leader. Enoder Niles played the cornet; well, but in the old-fashioned style, depending on his 'tipping', and getting quite at sea when it came to managing the valves. Bill Hawken was a beautiful, though untrained, euphonium-player. Tom Eplett's instrument was the 'bumbardon'. Once they went to play at a dance. One item in their repertoire was a galop which had a vocal trio. Will Charles, then a soprano, sang it. After the performance the paymaster came round. When he reached Eplett he slipped an extra shilling in his hand, and complimented him on the way he manipulated the bombardon in the accompaniment to the voice: 'You were putting it in as plum as biled turnips,' he said.

In Reuben's early days, hares were many, but rabbits were few; excluding the warren, not a thousand in the parish. Now six hundred in Winsor alone.

10. The Rosevear family, Parc Eglos, Mawgan

January 13th. Of an exhausted fighter: 'Couldn't blaw nor strike'. 'Kay Obb' at the inn last night with 'Suss Cayzer'. Kay is rabbit trapping, he and his brother, and, since yesterday, a third man. They teel three hundred gins, or more. Kay gives seventeen-pence apiece for his gins, which is reckoned dear. You can get good traps at thirteen-pence wholesale. The farmer on whose land you trap is customarily allowed to take what rabbits he wants (in moderation) from the store. Rabbits sent away twice or thrice a week. Never meddle with a spring gin in the dark. Suss did once, and found he had a rat by the tail.

January 15th. A Mawgan man, returning from the metropolis, complained that he couldn't see London for the houses – a variant of the old saying of the wood and the trees.

January 17th. Mrs Roberts' party, when they talked jam. Old Mrs Vivian totters to her feet, and grasps the mantelpiece, complaining of cramp, which she puts down to her hostess's preserves: ''Tis the sour and the sweet, my dear; the sour and the sweet.' Mrs Roberts' indignation. Never before had anybody breathed a word against her jam. Sour? How was that possible when her invariable rule was to put a pound of sugar to a pound of fruit, no matter *what* fruit it might be. The weight of the jam would prove her assertion. So she fetched in a mighty jar or pipkin, and passed it round for the company to guess its weight. Miss Gilbert thought it well to soothe her with a compliment. Now Mrs Roberts was accustomed to anoint her tresses profusely with castor oil, so that they shone like a porpoise's hide. So: 'How beautifully shiny your hair is, Mrs R.,' said she. 'Ess,' said Mrs R, drawing herself up. ''Tis written in Scripture that the righteous shall shine.'

January 19th. Shingles, wildfire, or, as it was called, 'wilfire', was once very prevalent here, and a certain old woman was famous for charming it. Another old dame was a noted serpent charmer. She declared that she could take an adder, set it on a board on the ground, and draw a circle round it with chalk, and that adder would be unable to stir till set of sun. But after sundown the spell could work no longer. One still alive saw the experiment tried, and sure enough the adder remained quiescent till the moment of sunset, when off it darted into the bushes.

Old Mr Vivian had a trick of talking to himself. One day, just before the annual court dinner, a labourer heard sounds in the stable and peeped in. There was V. applauding a rehearsal of his own speech, clapping his hands and exclaiming 'Brayvo.' 'Well spoke, Mr Vivian.' 'Best speech I ever heard in my life', etc.

He would brew a cask, a big ''orgate' (hogshead) of March ale for use at harvest.Then he would get *queels* (quills) and imbibe, letting the quills drop through afterwards. When harvest-time came, V. would have a barrel of quills.

Eight shillings a week was a labourer's wages fifty years ago.

Eight Newquay men bought a Bedruthan wreck, broke it up, tramping to and fro for a week, and thought themselves lucky to have £1 each in pocket.

The word for a man who goes about buying dairy produce to sell to dealers is a *regrator*.*

January 20th. 'Mr Hawken, you're the best hand at carving a goose that ever I seed.'

'Ess, well, en't bad; but I'll tell 'ee the principal part o' carving a goose. Always put a slice in under the carkess for yourself.'

H. used to go courting extensively in his youth; not so much for love of the maidens as to fill the vacancy caused by his own enormous appetite. He courted the Rectory

---

*This word is found as early as the fourteenth century for a buyer-up of dairy produce, eggs and fruit.

servants *passim*; and it was 'Look maidens, if you don't get me a bottle of wine next time, I don't come here no more.'

Gardener May last night: 'What's that striking? Nine o'clock. Only nine. What's wrong with the time down here that it is so slow? If I lived here, I shouldn't be so old as I be by a long way.'

Old Vivian holding forth in the inn kitchen, seated on a mangle. Somebody gives the handle a quiet turn, and imprisons his coat-tails; he unconscious of this till he rises to depart. He is the courtliest of old gentlemen – bare-headed when conversing with women, no matter who or where.

At Aunt's wedding-feast (many years ago) five snails were found in the broccoli, and Aunt was so upset that she burst into tears.

January 21st. Yesterday, the Carnanton Court Dinner at the Falcon. Thirty-seven tenants sat down with the two stewards, and ate a thirty-pound joint of roast beef, twenty pounds of boiled, three geese, four plum-puddings, and fruit and kickshaws.

One tenant present, a Mr Trebilcock, was within three weeks of his ninety-first birthday. This is the sixtieth court he has attended. His health was drunk with enthusiasm.

The speeches were cheerful enough, for last year was the best farmers have known for a long time. Joe Hawken was persuaded to sing, and gave us 'Blue-eyed Mary' – eyes to ceiling, thumbs in armholes of his waistcoat. Poaching yarns, too, by Hawken, whose outstrteched arms moved over the table, his fingers playing tattoos all the while. Of a wonderful greyhound bitch who would catch pheasants on the wing, leaping upon them as they rose in the air.

January 22nd. Reuben says of one: 'He was an 'anointer" – a modification of 'an anointed limb' (of Satan). He speaks of a widow's streamers as a '*single* of distress'. He uses '*romancing*' as a euphemism for swearing. Also 'He gave the whole *pedigree*' – went through the whole story.

January 23rd. 'I've come a-courting ov 'ee,' says Philip to Miss Hawken over to Polgreen. 'You'm the maid for me from the busket to the piano.' And later: 'What lovely teeth you've got, Miss Hawken.'

'Well, so they ought to be. Dad paid six pound for them.'

She is the drudge of the house. On Sunday evenings she works until near church time, then slips on her best dress, comes home after the service, slips off her feathers again, and milks half a dozen cows. Her famous Sunday hat has a bare quill sticking vertically twelve inches out of the top of it. Once there was another that protruded horizontally in front, but that got broken.

Why doesn't Miss Hawken get a young man? She isn't going to search for one, or hang about after church. There she is; they know where she lives and her road home; if they want to come after her they may.

January 25th. Of *frail*, the dialect word meaning a carpenter's large limp bag, or a smaller one for shopping: 'The Geneva or Breeches Bible of 1560 states that Abigail presented to David a hundred *frailles* of raisins.'

January 31st. Referring to our anthem, Mendelssohn's 'Hear My Prayer', in which the parts enter one after another and are singing different phrases most of the time, young Sam Lobb drew on his trade for a metaphor. 'It's a cross-grained piece,' said he – not meaning the phrase in the evil sense which commonly attaches to it.

Mem. The labourer who came to Dr Mackay and complained that he had lost his appetite, couldn't relish his food. As much as he could do to get down a pound and a half of beefsteak daily.

February 3rd. Local saying: 'As rough as Roughtor' (pronounced Rowter).

Mrs Sam Brewer, now lying dangerously ill with a three-day-old baby beside her, is a woman of some cultivation. Came here as a schoolmistress, and married a farmer. 'Out of place,' says Mrs Davie, 'a drawing-room wife.' Before she married she wouldn't get a cup of water for herself: now she is a drudge and a voluntary one, for Sam has told her time after time that he desires her to keep a couple of servants, as they can well afford to do. The doctor diagnoses her complaint as 'too much work, not enough to eat, and too many children' (there are eight now). 'They live like gypsies,' says Mrs D. The horse's harness hangs directly over the dinner table in the kitchen.

Charlie Lobb is famous for the amount of parcels he can pile into his little trap. Mrs D. describes it returning from Newquay 'piled up like a pagoda'.

February 5th. 'And Pal was *creening*' – whining excitedly, says Philip Gilbert. He describes Mr Crook, muffled up against the cold, as 'like a *fillfer* (fieldfare) after a fortnit's frost with its feathers all swelled out.'

February 7th. Jefferies, in his *Wild Life in a Southern County*, has some speculating on the ancient hill-top forts that crown the summits of the Wiltshire downs; and he asks the difficult question: How did the defenders obtain water? The same question might be asked concerning our Cornish cliff castles.

February 9th. Going into Rosevear's last night, found the parlour full of smoke. Reuben quoted:

> 'A smoking house and a scolding wife,
> Better a poor fellow were dead than a life.'

Of Leah Lobb's sweetheart, who was discarded because he got drunk one night at the inn. Stable man at Nanskival. Seen home by Edwin and a girl. Two hours on the way, cursing and blessing his maid. Confusion of identity. 'I ain't Jack Widgery; I'm Reuben Stick of Crantock.'

'Do I know where the key's to? I should think I d-did. I know several places where the key's to'.

'N-never was d-drunk in my life; but I-I'm d-d-darned near it now.'

February 10th. An American yarn: of one who fired at an immense flock of passenger pigeons as they rose from the ground, and fired just a second too late, and didn't kill one, but gathered a bushel and a half of severed legs.

February 11th. Reuben R., speaking of the proper way to

11. The Falcon Inn, on the left, Mawgan, *c.* 1890

manage some shrub, remarks, 'Plenty of people that know good ale, but don't know so much after that.'

February 12th. There is a local charity here; a Christmas dole secured on the rent of a couple of cottages. One clause in the deed is to the effect that no 'wrecker' is to receive any benefit from it.

Art Niles, describing the effect of frost on mason-work. 'First the fresh mortar freezes, and then when the frost is over, it thaws, and your work goes all abroad like a bag of mussels.'

February 14th. 'Three frosty mornings and then a flood o' rain; that's an old observation,' said the roadmaker.

The frequent occurrence and recurrence of certain local names – Tolcarne, Trenance, Porth . . . twice or thrice in the same parish – points to the isolation of village from village, town-place from town-place. If it had been necessary often to distinguish, distinction would have been embodied in the names. Now, with freer movement, confusion often arises: 'Where been?' 'Tolcarne' – which Tolcarne?'

'Mother was finely vexed – in a fine poor temper sure enough' – where *fine* answers to the West Cornwall *brave*.

Jack Kent at the inn yesterday begs for a pint, which he will pay for in the evening. At present he has only a ha'penny in his pocket. It is his rule to keep a ha'penny back; the rest goes to the missus. 'But what's the use of a ha'penny Jacky? You can't do much with a ha'penny.'

'Aw, yes you can; you can buy a orange with a ha'penny. I often buy a orange. Why, when I went for a soldier, I sailed all the way from England to India with nothing but a 'apenny in my pocket. No, I didn't nuther, come to think ov ut, I spent that 'apenny at Malta.' 'What did you buy with it?' 'A orange.' Jacky, employed in a rick-yard with the thrasher, is late in starting. 'Off I went, singing like the wind.' 'What did you sing?' 'Hold the fort for I am coming.'

February 15th. Mrs Brewer on the grand funerals that have come out of Carnanton. That of the late Mrs Brydges Willyams, engineered by men from Criddle and Smith, who 'looked fine' in new black suits and white aprons and – oh marvel! snowy white shirt-sleeves.

That of old Humphry Willyams, the wicked squire. As

it came down the village, a terrible storm broke, and a tremendous clap of thunder made the horses rear and scream. 'The gates of hell opening,' said the wise men of the village. No storm at St Columb; a purely local affair, and stage-managed by Providence for the occasion.

The old squire was very 'gay'.* Driving here with his wife, he ordered the coachman to stop at the door of a certain house. The man respectfully refused. He would not insult his mistress so. Naturally he was dismissed on the spot.

Mrs Brewer on music is always comic. They were very musical at her native Lostwithiel. She played the piano in the string band there, and they didn't perform cake-walks and Sousa as the St Columb band did, but good music – Haydn and Adagios and Andantes. Why, very often she would have as much as sixteen bars rest!

On Saturday night I went up into the belfry and watched the ringing. The various attitudes and gestures and expressions of the performers were interesting to watch. All intent, silent, rapt. One or two faces were changed out of recognition, notably that of young Dick Beswetherick, who with parted lips and fixed eyes, seemed to be seeing celestial visions. The oldest and most experienced, Joe Rawlins, scarcely moved, except for his hands and arms. Bolt upright, an almost imperceptible swaying of the body down to the hips. Dick bent his knees almost to a right angle at every stroke. John Walters doubled his body like a pair of compasses. Young Sam Lobb was perhaps the most

---

*At this date, *gay* means 'licentious', but with no suggestion of homosexuality.

graceful, swaying and bowing slightly; no effort, but no detachment from the rope.*

A youngster had a lesson, pelted by the critics all the while. 'Feel the bell,' was the *mot d'ordre*. The tendency is to pull too hard. The *fellet* must be caught firmly near the bottom; the hands must not slip along it.

Presently they had changes; young Sam calling them out of his head, according to his fancy. His difficulty, as he explained to me afterwards, is that the team will ring with their eyes, and not as they should with their ears. So instead of simply naming the bell that is to change places, and leaving the others to fall into line, he has to call all six each time: 'five to two, three to six, four to one', or whatever it is; and the followers face about and take their turn from the leaders' ropes, pulling a moment after if the two bells are near in the scale, but simultaneously if it be a heavy bell following a light one, because then the different widths of the bell-mouths are sufficient to ensure the proper interval.

The signal for preparing to ring is 'Go'; for starting, 'Gone'; for leaving off, a stamp of the foot from the leader. A pretty sight to see a good ringer mastering his bell in the *finale*. The signal for the final quickening is 'Down'.

A good peal, or rather 'touch', to end up. Noted the sounds. Four of the bells had longer ropes than the other two, so that the coils rapped the floor at each pull. There was this quadruple tap, there was the rustle of the ropepassing through its hole (the fellet hole) in the ceiling overhead, and the call of the bells themselves.

*Worked up into the episode of the ringing contest in *Dorinda's Birthday*.

Strongman, the steam thrasher, waiting in the inn kitchen for Philip, watches the preparation of a meal for the guest of the house. His amazement at seeing a mutton chop cooked like a pilchard on a gridiron. His thrifty soul disgusted at the waste. Not *his* way; much better 'put 'en in the frying-pan and 'lev 'en soakie in the fat'.

When the meal was cleared away, he was there to see the dishes carried out. 'Well, S., how did the lady get on with her dinner?' 'Well, she finished all o' wan chop, and a brave bit of bread, and every lick o' the soup.'

His father was a miser and skinflint and ill-treated his wife. On a rainy market-day a farmer took pity on her and offered her a lift home. 'That's right,' said S., 'step in, Jane, and get homealong, and mind you change your wet clothes for dry wans the minute you get in.' When they were out of hearing, poor Jane turned to the farmer, 'The lying villen – saying that, when he knaw I haven't a rag to wear but what I stand up in.'

'Half a crim' – a *crim* is a very small distance, measurable in inches. Of another old miser who counted his grains. When corn was being carried about, his starved chickens would wait at the door for stray grains. They would dart in, seize a morsel and dart off. Then it was: 'Jack, there goes the old cock with a head o' corn. After 'en', and a determined chase to recover the precious booty. When corn was being ground, he would be on the watch all the while to keep the miller from 'tolling' more grain or 'grice' than was his due. The miller's manoeuvre: going outside to see that the wheels were working properly, he would unhitch the old man's horse, and tell him five minutes later that the beast had got away. He after it, and the miller to take toll. Precisely the same trick is played by the miller in Chaucer's 'The Reeve's Tale'.

Another miller, 'Honest John', could always cheat a man, he said, but a boy's sharp eyes was another matter. So he kept his old muzzle-loader handy, and it was 'Look, my boy; there's an old blackbird in the hedge up the moor; you can take the gun and go fire to 'en if you like.' The bait took in nineteen cases out of twenty.

I note that these north-country folk, unlike the fishermen of the south,are little acquainted with the points of the compass. It isn't 'Sou'-wester blowing, we shall have rain', or the like, but 'I heard the Mawgan bells' or 'the St Eval bells this evening; wet day' or 'fine day tomorrow'. Or the roar of the sea, sounding from Newquay way or from Padstow way, as the case may be, is taken as a guide. The names of the winds are little used.

Looked in to see Ernest Richards, who was huddled over the fire, groaning with earache. In the night, says Polly, he was *'roving with the pain'*. She spoke of a visitor 'from St Dennis up'.

Mem. The sudden uproarious amusement of Rosevear's boy when I said I was on my way to jot down some bars of blackbird music.

February 19th. Local etymology. *Bolventor*, a lonely farm on a bleak eminence, so called because it was a bold venture to build in such a position.

Old tale of the first wagon that penetrated to North County, above Redruth. An excited crowd followed it, waiting to see the big wheels behind overtake the little wheels in front. All their sympathy with the little uns. Their

12. Lawry's Mill, Mawgan, *c*.1900

apprehension when the waggon turned a corner, and the inner front wheel seemed in danger of being run over. This from Reuben this afternoon.

February 23rd. There are choughs at Trevarrian, says Tom Eplett; generally some to be seen about the headland on the Newquay side of Livelow. Immediately after the protective notice was put up on the cliffs, he found one caught in a rabbit-trap – its legs broken. So Philip found his ring-ouzel.

To anger Higman the butcher, ask if he ever shot a woodcock. He once shot what he declared was a wood-cock, but it was an owl.

Of one up St Merryn way, on whom countless tricks are played, and more told of. Someone gets into his pigsty one night and whitewashes his pig. He comes round in the morning and *cooses* the strange porker, as he thinks it, down the road.

The Hawkens, father and son, Joe and Jim, their artfulness at a bargain. They take an ailing bullock to market and tie it up; then Joe strolls off. A stranger comes along, begins to bargain and hesitates. Up strolls Joe, and addresses his son, 'Excuse me, young man, but when you've finished with that gentleman?' 'In a minute, sir.' He slips off a little way, and hovers anxiously. Back again. 'If that gentleman don't want the bullock, I could do with him and half a dozen like him at the price.' The fish bites at once.

February 27th. Feast day approaching, Mrs Rosevear's thoughts turn to new garments. She goes to St Columb, where a prettily patterned though rather conspicuous stuff takes her fancy; she buys a length and makes it into a blouse. Feast day comes, and forth goes Mrs Rosevear, well-pleased with her attire. The first person she meets is Mrs George, with a complete gown of the same material. Then Mrs Jay, be-bloused in the same way; Mrs Hawkey similarly gowned; all alike. The worst of these germs of narrative is that they contain only the central situation, and you want a denouement as well. It would hardly do to make the Mawgan Maenads tear the traitorous draper into snippets.

Fred England tells how he came home leaking wet, and bade his wife make up the fire so that he might dry his clothes. 'She didn' say nothing, but just took up the tay-pot and throwed it at me. Tay-leaves all over me. So I said "Your place, missus, is outside the door." And I put her out and I locked her out.'

Miss Gilbert, at the Falcon Inn, has taken to india-rubber shoes. Her noiseless movements are not to the taste of Mrs Davie, who suggests ferret bells about her sister's neck.

Janie's three brothers sleep in one bed. 'Some row some-times. Wan like a sheet, the other like a blanket.' What the third likes is not recorded.

At St Columb church there is, or was, a door leading outside from behind the organ. Old Berryman the organist and his blower never waited for the sermon, but slipped out, Berryman to have a glass of something, the blower to 'het' the oven for dinner. Timed the sermon, and were back for the last hymn.

1903–1908

Mawgan-in-Pydar, London
Gorran Haven

March 3rd. We met Granny. 'There, I knowed how 'twould be if I put this bistly old apron on, I'm sure to meet a lady-an-gen'lman.' Then, an explanation: she was getting water from the 'shute', and she didn't like to use the water that stood in the stone trough, so she put her can under the shute itself, first removing the section of 'launder' – and to do this she had to lean against the trough, all muddy and green with moss.

Of Jack Kent, getting uproarious in a farm kitchen, so that nobody had a chance of a word with his neighbour. Farmer's wife promises a pint if he will remain silent till the clock on the chimney points to nine (the hands then standing at 8.45). J. promises, and waits, and waits and waits. 'Sim'me the old clock's terrible slow, eh Jacky?' A nod with pursed lips, and so on, till J. begins to doubt. Three quarters of an hour at least, and those hands haven't advanced an inch. At last he bursts out in wrathful speech. 'You've lost your pint,' – and somebody slily pushes the hands on, and Jacky is left lamenting.

March 7th. Reuben on Mawgan farmers, old style and new. The wealth, if you go back, contrasted with the poverty of today. Partly due to increase of expenses and wages; but 'that place below' is held mostly responsible. Several fortunes lost in drink. Mr May's father spent ten shillings a day at the inn for years. Gilbert senior (a former landlord) standing drinks, and being stood the same: ostensibly drinking brandy, but really cold tea, so that he remained sober while his victims grew more and more reckless of their cash.

Of one who, drawing a large sum in gold, walked through St Columb streets from one bank to the other carrying the money in his box, or 'long-sleeve', hat – a white one with a black brim. This out of pride and ostentation.

March 9th. Last night, our weekly yarn at the Rosevears'. Tom Eplett in good form.

Reuben Rosevear began life as a farm apprentice on 'twelve shilling a year and a lacing' (good hiding).

Saying, of one who is a 'good fellow out and brute home' is 'He hang his fiddle outside the door'.

Of the Withiel parson, one of the Vyvyans. He goes into the blacksmith's shop. 'Joe,' says he, 'I'm going to ask you a straightforward question, and I want you to give it a plain, straightforward answer.' 'Well, sir, I'll do so if I can.' 'The question is this, whom do you consider to be the biggest blackguard in this parish?' Jim's eyes twinkle, he scratches his head, and feigns embarrassment. 'That's a terrible hard question, sure 'nough . . . You see, 'tis a big parish . . . Well, I don't know . . . Aw, I don't know, sir: I'd as soon say 'twas the parson as anybody else.' 'A very good answer,' chuckles Vyvyan.

One Steve Langdon here was famed for his power of extempore rhyme. An old lady, Mary X, was ill, and fancied herself dying. She summoned Steve: 'Mr Langdon, I'm going to die tonight.' 'Are 'ee sure, Mary? Well, you don't look like it.' 'Yes, I be; and Mr L, I want 'ee to write some poetry about my dying.' 'Aw, don't know.' 'Do, now.' 'Well, I'll try.' 'To wance - I'd like to see that poetry 'fore die.' Steve retired within himself for a few moments, and came out again with 'How's this, missus?

> 'Holy Mary dies of late
> Safe arrived to Heaven's gate.'

'Aw, that's beautiful, Mr Langdon, beautiful.'
'Glad you d'like it, Mary, but wait a bit; must have another two lines to finish 'en off fitty. Lemme see: How's this?

> 'Up come Satan with his club,
> Knocked her down to Beelzebub.'

On that, the old dame forgot her moribund state, leapt from her bed, and drove him from the house.

There is a lady from Trevarrian who 'speaks lipsy', as they say in Cornwall. She is chapel-going, but not a teetotaller: 'I baint no drinker, but I alwayth taketh a li'll bottle o' gin to chapel. I do thuffer terrible with painth in the thtomach, and if I didn' take my li'll bottle o' gin to chapel, where'd I be if the painth should hap to come on in the middle o' the dithcourthe.'

She had a sweetheart, a profane drunken rascal, who got six months hard. The maid gets letters from him, and is delighted to find he's improving: he never misses a service, he writes, and he hasn't got drunk once.

The old man who was walking in front of me into Trevarrian the other day was 'Cute', Happy Dick's brother, a notorious wrecker. Tom Eplett met him last week: he is Tom's tenant, and trusts him. 'Any wreck?' 'Well . . . ' in a whisper, 'don't mind telling 'ee . . . got a couple o' bags o' flour in a cavie – rolled flour from Swansea – seventy pound in aich bag that the water haven' got to. But you won't say a word, will 'ee?' Tom swears secrecy, and Cute moves on, and meets another man, also a 'terrible wrecker'. Says he, 'Well, any wreck?' 'Haven' seen none,' says Cute. 'I reckon the wind's too far out.' The other man joins Tom. 'Hear that? The old rogue. I could see his back all white where he'd been carr'ing the flour. I knowed very well. I'd had a bag o' that same flour before he set eyes 'pon it.'

Of parsons, and notably of the St Ervan parson, whose church-tower is falling, whose average congregation numbers three, who once blacked his wife's eye and then went off and preached a sermon; who, performing the marriage ceremony, said something aside against the bride's fair fame, and was promptly threatened with the bridegroom's fist: 'Say any more of that, mister, and I'll knack 'ee down.'

Of Olivey, the St Merryn parson, a fine speaker in the district council, and a sharp farmer into the bargain. Does all the rough work, carrying dressing, attending *accouchements* of cattle, etc. Swaggers about St Columb

Fair, his long tails flapping, boasting that his lambs are the finest lambs in the market. Mrs Perrin visits him, and he starts to drive her home in his neat little trap. She mounts. 'One moment' – he darts off into the house and returns with two buckets of pig swill, which he puts in beside her, and takes as far as his farm.

Of the late James Williams, who was over-gardener at the Convent, under a supine priest and an oblivious Mother Superior. He improved the opportunity in various ways: finally he began cutting down timber and selling it to his brother-in-law, who was building a ship at Newquay. £200 worth was thus disposed of, and nothing would have come to the authorities' ears, if James hadn't been too cautious, and sent a load away, not by the main road, but through Polgreen and Tolcarne. Curiosity was thus aroused, inquiries followed, and James got the sack.

He didn't overwork himself, but spent much of his time at the Inn. White waistcoat, jet watch-chain to his gold watch. Swaggering out one day when strangers were about, he was greeted by a humorist with: 'Why, Jim, where's your apron?' Jim collapsed like a pricked bladder. Of James it is recorded, that being employed on a job up at Tolcarne, he went up daily in his black visiting suit, carrying his mason's garb in a *frail* and changing in an outhouse after arriving and before departing.

Joe Hawken was persuaded by parson to come to communion. The cup was offered; he drank. 'Very good stuff, sir; I shouldn't mind a drop more.'

'Aunt' rushed in to the Rosevears' at ten o'clock on Saturday morning to tell them that the Drew scandal had no foundation, or at least had been smoothed over. Mr

Powell had told her that Mr D. had been 'down on his hands and knees' to his wife, to tell her that he had nothing to do with the maid.

Postman Trembath, met by Dick Beswarick. 'Fine morning, Mr T.'

'Ugh! There's another ov 'em. Fine morning! As if I couldn' see for myself 'twas a fine morning.' He told me on Saturday he had been driving against the head wind 'for a fortnight'. He has to clear the Watergate box in the afternoon. When, as often happens out of season, there isn't a letter in it, it's positively dangerous to accost him. Going up the hill to Tregurrian, it's useless to attempt to stop him. If you have a letter to post you must trot up behind, and deliver it at the box.

This is the twelfth anniversary of the blizzard, when, as Happy Dick says, it blizzarded down beach and blizzarded up tap o' th' hill.

Of hurling. The final hurl in St Columb on Saturday. The town won, not by putting the ball into goal, but by carrying it out of the parish to St Dennis. The ball weighs nine and a half ounces, with a core of apple-wood, coated with copper and over that with beaten silver. Its size is between a cricket and a tennis ball. The 'silver ale', drunk by the winner, is a jug of ordinary ale, in which the ball is soused before drinking.

March 11th. Jim Hawken notes how the chaps are always going around with the maids, and he can't understand it. He has squired several maids in his time, but got no profit or entertainment thereby. He may have been unlucky, but it's a fact that every one of these maids suffered in her feet with corns or bunions or the like, which spoiled their action. He wouldn't go so far as to say they were foundered, but 'twas a case of cracked heels with them, and no mistake. Now when he was last up Wadebridge way he was noticing some fine dry upland pastures, and he thought to himself 'twould be a good plan now and again to turn out all the women in the parish to grass on that land, for a fortnit, say. The men would enjoy a brief fore-taste of heaven, and the women would return sound in wind and limb.

Reuben on the old days. He wishes they would return for a month, that the young generation might see what they were like. When he and two others were working on a farm, their invariable supper was salted pilchards from the barrel. Missus would go down to the cellar and fetch up thirty – never more or less – ten pilchards to each mouth. 'Yes,' said Tom. 'I've heard how the gulls used to coose you in they days.'

Up this street we pride ourselves on our respectability. We may have unauthorised babies, but we never allow anyone, as they do over to Shop, to be seen in the road with an apron on. Mrs James Charles puts on kid gloves to fetch the milk.

March 20th. Mrs Kestle, it is said, always keeps a pan of dirty water handy, and ready for the advent of strangers – not to throw over them, but so that she may have a colourable excuse for going to the door to take stock of them.

Of a singing contest in the West, where a young gipsy boy enraptured all with his sweet voice. It was a common music-hall song he sang, but he sang so well as to tie for first prize. Then the tie was sung off, and the innocent Romany trolled forth the only other song he knew, a tavern catch, unfit for ladies' ears. To his amazement he was bundled out of the hall at the end of the first verse.

Miss Houghton, the disorganised Mawgan shopkeeper, ordered no fewer than twenty trimmed hats from London; and now she and Emma can't sleep a wink o' nights, fearing they may fail to dispose of them. Nor is she sure where to put them. The shop is full, the parlour is full, the attics and bedrooms are full, the very oven is full, and cooking is done on a little oil stove in the shop.

March 26th. My wife has been to see the hats: 'You'll have many admirers,' said she. 'Well, perhaps,' said Miss Houghton, 'but they won't come to see *me*, they'll come to see the hats.' Neither she nor her assistant Emma have ever travelled by rail. Once they were going to Plymouth, but at the last moment the expense and waste of time caused them to pause; and instead, they stayed at home and sat up all night over their accounts.

March 28th. Miss Houghton has disposed of thirteen out of her twenty hats already. Mawgan, she remarks, is getting more and more like London every day; but then Miss Houghton has never been to London. I went into the shop the other day for cheese. Emma must be summoned to decide whether the cheese was fit for consumption by the gentry, and also to find the cheese, which was brought out of the parlour. Miss H. had heard that Mr Lee means to write about her. She hopes he will remember that she has

13. Rose Cottage, Tregurrian, Mawgan, 1926

just added a new branch to her business, and that the shop is rather untidy in consequence. The cheese is weighed. An ounce over the half pound. 'Shall we say fourpence ha'penny, Emma?' Emma assents.

Miss Houghton intends to come to church, though a Dissenter, to hear Mr Lee's playing. She tells the Wesleyans that they must find better preachers if they want to keep her. Mr Wayne a good preacher? She must judge for herself in that matter. Reads his sermons? She doesn't mind, so long as his discourse is thoroughly evangelical.

Mrs Brewer's dogs slipped into church with her last Good Friday. They were quiet and unobserved, till they saw her kneel, bow her head, and hide her face in her hands. Then, conceiving her to be in distress, they lifted up their voices in sympathy.

March 30th. Reuben on the old days once more. There was a man of St Merryn who when he was in funds would walk over to Mawgan in his shirtsleeves and stay here drinking till his money was spent. It might be a fortnight; and then he would start home. At Trevedras Water a fumble in a forgotten pocket; a coin discovered; it might be a sixpence, it might be a sovereign; but anyway, 'halt, right about face, quick march' – back to the Inn.

Tricks on an old lady returning from church in the dark, past Shop. At the river a match lit: 'This way, mum', and the confiding dame walks straight into the water.

Of robbing orchards. For proper enjoyment it is essential that you should be *coosed*. The fruit was safe when the farmer was away or in bed.

In Captain Hunt's days it was impossible to keep a cat.

He paid his keepers sixpence a tail, and they were not particular whether the cat was found in the plantation or outside.

Mrs W. Cayzer has had a miscarriage. It is attributed to her having entered a room where the wife of one of her hinds had lately had a similar 'mishap'. The same superstition about horses: it is dangerous to put a breeding mare in a field where another mare has had an untimely birth.

April 7th. There was a coastguardsman here who was courting Miss Daniels, the ex-schoolmistress; and also at the same time a local milliner. He hesitated between the two. One day he was observed holding a pair of scissors in one hand and a pen in the other, and earnestly contemplating those symbols. After a long consideration he resolutely cast the pen down on the table, and went out and forthwith proposed to the dressmaker.

Of one Libby, who caught cold the other day, and went to see the doctor. 'Don't know how I come to catch 'en. Either 'twas through sleeping with my mouth abroad, or else 'twas drinking out of a damp cup'. Doctor gave him some *trade*, and told him to take it in water. Next day a wayfarer found him up to his middle in a duck pond, bottle in hand. 'Doctor told me to take it in water, and I thought the deeper I went in the more good it 'ud do me.'

One advantage of being a ringer, says Boy Sam, is the freemasonry of the craft. Finding yourself in a strange village, you drop a remark about the bells, and a friend starts up at once.

Mrs Wayne tells of a church barrel organ in Wales in the days of her youth, which was liable to disorder. On occasion, being started, it would get out of control, and would not stop until it had ground out the whole repertoire.

Reuben on the old days. The timber ploughs of his boyhood. The first Scotch plough. The first wheeled plough, forty-five years ago. Reuben made a Sunday excursion to see 'the plough that go by itself'. Then the first scythe or 'sigh'. Before that they 'hewed' or 'reaped'. In hewing you let the wheat fall and lie; in reaping, you gathered a handful and struck at the massed stalks. The hewing-hook was wider or more open than the reaping-hook. The first attempt to use a scythe. Prejudice against it: 'No sighs in my field.' 'Never do,' as the novice stumbled, and dug his blade into the ground, nearly cutting off his own legs.

John James' 'dunkey' greedily devouring ramson (wild garlic) or 'ramsay' as it is called here. The Polgreen butter is uneatable just now. And from this time up to Michaelmas the trappers leave the Lanherne rabbits severely alone, their flesh being rank with garlic. A local preacher discoursing of the Israelites finds in his heart an excuse for them when they tired of manna, manna, manna, breakfast, dinner and supper, and longed after the flesh-pots of Egypt 'with a brave handful of ramsay into 'em'.

Of the present St Ervan parson. Years back, when prayers for rain were still offered, a farmer asked him to put one up next Sunday. 'Not a bit of good till the wind shifts,' said he.

Of Olivey, the present St Merryn parson, on his way to the chancel, stooping to a farmer in a pew, and asking in a loud whisper, 'Has the fly got into your turnips yet?'

The fly is dangerous only to the young plants in drouth.

When rain comes, and the big rough leaves sprout, all peril is over.

April 20th. 'Bussy milk' is the first milk drawn from the cow after calving. Some children used to be fond of it; and it is sometimes used in making cakes. The first pailful is given to the cow as a drench (or 'drunch', as it is called here).

April 28th. Bill Hawken's story of a man, a Redruth calf-jobber, wounded in the leg in the South African War. Doctor set it. Three months' convalescence. Tries to walk, but finds the leg has been set 'forth and back'. He calls the doctor, and bids him bring a sledge-hammer and break the leg anew. This is done, the leg is re-set right way round, and now the man is all right, except that he walks a bit bandy, instead of round in circles as before.

May 1st. Mrs Wayne tells ghost stories of Carnanton. There is a spectral coach. It manifested itself about a year ago. The family was having music after dinner, and it was getting near prayer-time – ten o'clock. The coach was heard to drive up to the door, the bell was rung, and the flap-flap-flap of the three steps being let down was distinctly heard. The servants went to the door, the old stable dog, who never came to the front except when visitors arrived, rushed out barking, and the gentlemen of the family, surprised at the late arrival, came out into the hall. The door was opened. Nobody there.

May 8th. Part of a field near Gallivane was known as Rick or Reck Park. Here was a blanket maker's. A *rick* or *reck* was a structure like a four-bar gate. These were set up one above another on the side of the hill, and *plats* (green plots) above them, and the blankets thrown over them. The hillside was cut into narrow terraces (? for the stretching and drying). Below was a house where the blankets were stored; known as Little Hell, because of the brimstone that was always being burned there. Old Parkyn was the blanket maker. He collected the village slop-water in pails (to make lye to wash the blankets in). He wore 'leatheren breeches and stockens down over 'es boots'.

A *visgey* is described as a cleaver on top of a pick. In cutting hedges, etc. you use the lower part with a sweeping blow; coming to a tough root you hack with the other part. It differs from a *twobeal*, which is more like a navvy's pick.

In the old days, at a christening, a big *groaning* cake was made and presented to the first person the party met when going to church. To keep it in the family, somebody was sent to sit outside the door.

Reuben can remember when many apprentices got as little as four shillings a year. Often they slept in an outhouse ('and then go to straw', as the saying was). Reuben's father came to Mawgan when three years old from Luxulyan. When the Roche venturers came over he, knowing the road, acted as guide. A favourite hiding-place for 'kags' was Watergate Mine. There would be thirty or forty men on a smuggling party, with horses and donkeys.

Feats of labour: mowing three fields between 10 p.m. and 5 a.m.; and then going off to work at Nanskival. R. did it, he and another, on a gallon of beer.

Reuben can 'mind' when a farmer wanting hands would apply to the overseers. Then, on Sunday evening, as the folk went out to church, the clerk would go to the gate and cry 'Oyez, Oyez', and the men would stand and be picked – 'You go to so-and-so.'

May 11th. A *journey* in the old days meant an allotted piece-work, carrying so many loads of manure, or spreading the same, etc. The old-time folk, gluttons for work, would accomplish a *journey* – nominally a day's work – by the time the children were starting for morning school.

A 'sparrow' is 'a double wooden skewer used in thatching'. One of the winter fireside occupations was sparrow-making. One would cut them, another split them, each roughly shaped piece of wood being divided into four sparrows, and another sharpen the ends. In thatching, it was essential that the sparrow should be thrust into the roof so as to slope upwards in the thatch, that the water might run down the exposed part; otherwise it would run into the thatch and rot it.

May 12th. Timber was scarce here, even within Reuben's recollection. There was a carpenter at Carloggas who, when he received an order for a washing-tray or coffin, would start off that night for Truro, purchase the necessary timber, and walk home with it on his back, twenty-eight miles in all. Reuben himself helped to 'rip the piece of ground' for several plantations. All the plantation above the drive, in the direction of Carloggas, was, in his young days, *tealed* to corn one year and to 'taties' the next. Cornfields all about Lawry's Hill, and the allotments. And there was a well, Jacob's Well, by the road . . . 'I was a little tagger then,' says Reuben.

As for *plow* in the sense of 'dray' or 'wain', there was an old man, Joe Rawlin's father, alive quite lately, who used the word. One of the Epletts asked him how the corn-carrying was going on: 'We had in two plows today,' said he.

Churching of women was regular; no respectable woman would omit it. It was known here as *uprising*. The seat where William Cayzer sits in church was the uprising seat. When a man put in an appearance at church who was not wont to be seen there, it was said jokingly 'He's uprose'.

May 14th. Dick B. uses the expletive 'By goles'.

Dung forks made by blacksmiths. A job to get them in to the manure; a bigger job to get them out.

'She d'get round he like a hoop round a treacle cask,' says Reuben.

May 21st. On Tuesday last an entertainment with tableaux, etc., and the new song 'Mawgan Church Town' – a great success.* But the mother of Emma (Miss Houghton's assistant), who is a strict Wesleyan, objects. Very carnal behaviour, going to Church, and then coming across and listening to a pack of lies. For it (the song) was mostly lies, by what she hears. But there'll be a day of reckoning: 'They'll be weighed in the balance and found wanting. You know that so well as I do.'

Policeman is proud of his distinctive dog. He 'cooses' the hen round the house till he gets her in the corner. Then they fight and 'the hen's best man'. A capital watchdog. They daren't move any furniture; he will bark till it is

*Written by Lee.

put back in place. They took down a portrait of Lord Kitchener: he barked at the stern warrior for half an hour on end.

Up street they gossip all morning, forget to put in the rice pudding, and in consequence the poor old man has indigestion.

May 24th. The old custom of condemning an offender against certain rules of discipline to distribute bread at the church gate still prevailed within living memory. The bread was distributed on Sunday, from a cart by the lych-gate (though the lych-gate did not then exist). According to the magnitude of the offence, the fine would be £1 worth or less, or more up to £3 pounds worth. One Nicholl, still alive at Padstow, was condemned to £25 worth at St Columb. It takes time and labour to give away £5 worth, loaf by loaf. The criminal would get impatient, and begin throwing the loaves into the crowd, which was thickly massed. Then you would see a box-hat tip over, and knock down the box-hat behind it, and that the hat behind it again. Then the official would interfere. No throwing; each loaf must be handed out separately. £5 worth would take a couple of Sundays. Every parishioner entitled to a loaf.

Reuben has seen men in the stocks. One lately dead was the last to be put in, for swearing at a vestry meeting, 'damning them all into heaps'. The culprit was put in before morning service, and remained till the evening, with a crust and a jug of water to console him. All the small boys in the village gathered round and criticised. Where are the stocks now?

There was a hepping-stock before the church, on which the sexton would ascend after service, and cry things lost, pigs for sale, etc.

Currow was the 'shaft horse' in the ceremony of making a mayor of a drunken man. On a feast night you would see some twenty men and women lying dead drunk in the inn. Out would go C. to the stable, fetch the cart. A victim would be hoisted in, and off pranced Currow, like a spirited horse, to the great bridge, which then had no parapet. The cart was backed, and tipped: Splash! And back curvetted C. for a fresh victim. Returning, the cart would pass the other half way, dripping like a drowned rat. 'There's so-and-so,' says X., 'brave and drunk; think he's about ready. If he isn't exactly, I'll get in the cart and hold him. Only give me time to get out when we come to the bridge.' But they didn't, and both were soused.

Someone lost a pig. Gathered together a search party. Couldn't find the pig. Back to the Inn: gallons of ale: half the night in drinking. Search renewed next day: pig found. More drink. 'Another gallon, missus.' 'You can't: you've drunk up the pig.'

May 30th. Of the former tenant of Lanvean, old Thomas, whose oath was 'Christ Jay' and who would never keep a black or spotty pig, when a litter of *vears* or farrows was born. If they were anything but white they were killed, one and all.

June 3rd. The old land-measure here was the 'goad' (same word, according to the OED, as ox-goad). The goad for measuring is a rod nine feet in length. There were old men who with a goad, turning it over and over, could measure land as quickly and accurately as with a chain.

June 9th. About April a farmer in the old days would lay in a 'cave of turnips' – cutting off tops, etc., for the use of his labourers. One man hired himself to such a farmer, who fed him for a month on turnip pie, fried turnips, and on spinach and peppercress. At the end, he was asked, would he stay? He thought not. He'd been a fortnit in the house and a fortnit out to grass, and he reckoned he was fat enough to kill.

Styane in the old Mawgan papers = *stean*, which is the equivalent of mid-Cornwall *stug* [= *buzza*], West Cornwall *clome buzza*, an earthenware pot used for storing pilchards, butter, etc.

The peacock butterfly is here a King George.

Of the pews at St Merryn. Thirty or forty years ago, when corn was dear, there were well-to-do farmers there, and each built himself a private enclosure in the church. One would be polished mahogany, perhaps with a shining brass handle; another plain *dell*.

At one time, Squire Humphry quarrelled with Parson Stephens, and for years every Sunday he mounted his white pony and rode off to the Wesleyan Chapel at St Columb.

June 12th. Rode St Ervan way, a pretty pastoral country. Then went to Butcher Tonkin's to try his wonderful piano. Admiring some furniture, I was shown every chair and ornament in the room, and bidden to 'try their weights'.

For Butcher Tonkin chairs and candelabra are as bullocks –
their quality is measured in terms of avoirdupois.

June 15th. According to Reuben, there was a man
nicknamed 'Daffadilly' who used to attend Mawgan Feast.
Seated in a cart in front of the inn, he would eat fifty
pilchards and a leg of mutton, washing down the repast
with four gallons of ale.

In the old days, no black coats. Fustian was the wear. A
new coat did duty on Sundays till it showed signs of use:
then it was worn to market for a year or so: then it came
down to workaday use: then it went on the scarecrow.

Nicknames of places are as popular here as nicknames
of persons, and they have the same trick of supplanting,
even extinguishing, the real names. Thus Pollard's Hill is
now Blackbird's: and why? Because of one working there
who came to the farmer with news that he'd seen a
blackbird, and would have caught him if he hadn't flown
away.

June 25th. Mawgan Feast used to last a week; beginning on
Monday with donkey races at Trevarrian, and shifting to
Churchtown and wrestling on the Tuesday. Inn open
all night, and a hundred tipsy persons hallooing about.
Reuben's last serious visit to an inn was one Feast night
when he was young. A dozen times he started for home, a
dozen times a fresh uproar began and enticed him back. At
last, long after midnight, he fairly took to his heels and ran.
Since then (thirty years) he hasn't spent three shillings in a
pub. Reuben gives a list of those ruined at the inn. Reuben
and Richard Cobledick, who went to drink as they might

go to work; an hour or two in the morning, an hour in the afternoon, and all the evening. Fred May likewise; five morning goes, five afternoon, and who knows how many at night? Two grogs while another was blowing the froth off his beer. Fifteen shillings at St Columb in drink every market day. 'My fortune is there,' says another, pointing to the inn where his worthy father had spent his all.

Much from Reuben of old Squire Humphry: he was the sort of man who was 'always pulling down and building up.' Six workmen in continuous employment, and much road-making. When Lawry's Mill was working, and until a dozen years before it closed down, there were no roads into that valley, only bridle paths. Lawry's prosperity rose from a tragedy: a girl of the family got into trouble with the Squire and strangled herself. Reuben saw the butler carrying her out, hanging over his shoulder, her tongue protruding 'a foot long'. She was the first suicide to have Christian burial in these parts. The Squire moved heaven and earth to effect this. Squire helped the family.

Squire hated the police, and would have none of them. On the bench, he did his best to prevent conviction in a case where the police prosecuted. A police witness fared badly in his hands. There was a volunteer fête at Carnanton. His eagle eye espied a policeman in a top hat. Policeman explains that he is bound to be present where there are booths. 'Then go down by the booths and stay there.' And stay he had to till midnight.

June 27th. 'Taking off the top' of a pint of beer for a companion: supposed a courtesy, but the joker interprets 'top' very liberally: 'Shall I take off the top for 'ee again?' 'No thank 'ee – I want a drink this time.'

Aunt in her youth, afflicted with melancholy. They tried everything to cheer her up, and as a last resort took her to Bodmin to see an execution.

Of one who had a barometer; at harvest time it stood at set fair while the rain continued to pour. This went on for some days, he damning the glass right and left, till at last he unhooked it and took it to the door: 'Here – come outside and see for yourself.'

August 12th. Walked to St Columb to see the 'carnival' in the evening. Blacksmith's forge, maypole, cart full of niggers, patriotic cart, quack doctor, etc.- not bad for a small town.

August 15th. Mawgan Flower Show. The intending exhibitor, if he is wise, keeps a careful watch over his garden for a day or two before the show, or he may find his dahlias stripped, his broad beans stolen. Two years the first prize for apples was carried off by one who did not possess a single tree. He had gone round and taken the pick of his neighbours'.

September 9th. After a fortnight in London, we returned in time for the funeral of Mrs Stephens, sister of Squire Willyams, and widow of Ferdinand Stephens, formerly rector here. Taylor has tied a bit of crêpe on our beehive, to warn the inmates of Mrs Stephens' death. He used not to believe in the necessity for this, but when Mrs Arthur

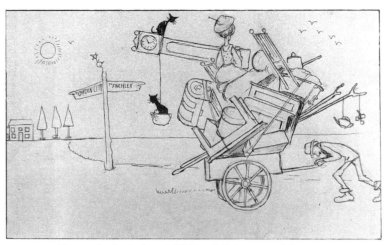

14. Cartoon by Lee's friend, W. Heath Robinson, of the novelist leaving London for Letchworth.

Willyams died, the bees were not notified, and a dozen hives languished and died.

October 6th. The belief that May cats bring vermin into the house is confirmed by Florence, our maid; she knows it to be so; adders they bring, and all manner of creeping things. It would seem that August cats have the same trick: Sambo our kitten was found the other day in the dining-room, foaming at the mouth, and attempting to eat a fine brown slug.

October 10th. Yesterday went down to Winsor with Reuben. The mill at work grinding corn. The charge is sixpence a bushel – the Cornish bushel, equal to three Winchester bushels. If the corn is dry, the mill can grind three such bushels in an hour. The crusher was also set to work on some 'dredge-corn', or mixed barley and oats. It will crush seven or eight bushels in an hour; charge, fourpence a bushel.

The mill works smoothly, to the delight of its owners, who are proud of their new toy. A regular triple click-*click*-click, which sounds to my ears like 'You *id*jut, you *id*jut'. This is caused by the 'Jenny', which a simple adjustment causes to vibrate below the hopper, so as to shake the corn in a regular stream into the hole in the upper mill-stone. When the hopper was empty, Reuben took it off, and worked the corn in the box below with his hand, so as to keep it flowing. Of course the speed of the stones increased as the trickle diminished. By rights, the hopper should not be taken off. The miller stops the stones as soon as the hopper is empty. What remains in the box is his perquisite.

The mill seems likely to prove profitable, since neighbouring farmers are tired of carrying their corn to St Columb and having to call day after day to get their meal.

October 11th. Old Sam Lobb, putting the brasses into the wall of the church, discourses on the restoration forty years ago, when he was hardly a man. When the contractors had gone it was he that gathered up the old oak they had left, and fitted it together. Some of the bench-ends were broken and mutilated, and he replaced the gaps with fresh carvings. A worthy successor of the master-carpenters of Mawgan, 500 years ago, who first carved them.

October 14th. Still it rains. This afternoon in the blacksmith's shop. William Richard Beswetherick and Ernest

Richards at work on the blade of a farm implement, welding a fresh piece of iron into it and shaping it anew. Interesting to watch Ernest wielding the big hammer, and Dick doing the artistry with the small one. A faint grunt from him at every blow. Now he turns the blade on edge in the interval between the other's blows, and strikes it here and there: now no blow is wanted, but he taps the anvil to keep up the rhythm. The water for tempering and cooling is in a trough let in under the forge. Bits of rejected metal are thrust into a pigeon-hole made in the side masonry of the forge. The sparks fly: I ask if no damage comes to their eyes. Seldom, but often they get burnt when a spark gets lodged in their sleeves or between the hand and the tool. Mrs Perrin once asked the same question, and laughed and laughed at the answer: 'We shut our eyes when we see the sparks come past our noses.'

October 17th. Reuben, before going off to '*mait* the pigs', tells this tale of his youth. He and another man were ploughing a field above Tolcarne, and there was a bitter North-East wind blowing. It was numbing work. Their horses were old stagers, so Reuben stationed himself under the hedge at one end of the field, his mate at the other, and they left the two teams to take the furrows of themselves, simply intervening to turn them at the ends. They lit a fire under the hedge, set up stones, and laid their pasties on the stones, across the fire, to warm. Suddenly, Master is seen coming along, They rush to their ploughs. When Master's gone, behold their pasties burnt to a cinder, and they are dinnerless.

October 22nd. Of two men, who came with a threshing machine to Winsor, in Hortop's days. They finished their work, had supper and went straight to bed in the empty house. After a long slumber they awoke. It was late autumn, when getting-up time is dark. What was the time? No watches. Wasn't there a clock hanging in the passage downstairs? Yes, to be sure, they had noticed a clock as they came in. One gets up, stumbles down stairs with a light, and consults the time-piece. Such a darned old clock he never set eyes on: couldn't make head or tail of the figures, but by the way the hands were pointing, he should say 'twas 'bout half past five. Time to pitch work. On with their clothes, fire lighted, and steam nearly up, when the convent clock strikes twelve. The 'darned old clock' was an aneroid barometer.

October 28th. No clocks, either, at Tolcarne in the old days. One cottager took his rising time from a rat who shared the house. 'Time to get up, father?' 'No, the rat haven't gone yet.' Another asks the time, explaining that his watch is twenty-four hours slow, he having put the key in the wrong key-hole and turned the hands back instead of winding the spring up.

November 2nd. In those days, as Reuben remembers them, the shoemaker would go about from farm to farm. The farmer bought *taps* and leather, and the cobbler would spend a day or two or more, mending the footgear of the establishment. At one farm he stayed 'up a fortnit'. Ready money was scarce; would the cobbler take a pig in payment? He agreed, on at least one occasion.

The Sentries are the fields between Carloggas and Lawry's, where the 'stile-road' goes. One at St Merryn has ruined walls in it (of a chapel?), close by where Parson Olivey keeps his pigs. *Sentries* are said to be a corruption of *sanctuaries*.

[In November, Lee left Mawgan for London; but kept being reminded of the village throughout the next year, 1904.]

July 1st. With the Serpentine Dance* of Mawgan Feast, compare the choric dance (Cretan?) of youths and maidens depicted on Achilles' shield in Homer's *Iliad*.

[Lee quotes Chapman's translation:]

> Sometimes all wound close in a ring, to which at last
>   they spun
> As any wheel a turner makes, being tried how it
>   will run
> While he is set; and out again as full of speed
>   they wound,
> Not one left fast or breaking hands. A multitude
>   stood round,
> Delighted with their nimble sport.

July 13th. I never picked a harebell or a cowslip in Cornwall.

---

*This strange dance, which I have taken part in, seems to be, or to have been, peculiar to mid-Cornwall. Variously called the Snail-creep and (by Lee) the Snake-walk, it is described in the ninth chapter of *Dorinda's Birthday*. It is a great pity that the old custom should have been so recently allowed to die.

August 25th. The Cornishman's love of abstract argument –
surely a rare trait among peasantry outside Celtdom.

September 23rd, 1907. Mawgan phrases: R.R. uses *outrider**
for 'commercial traveller'. 'To go down stream' means 'to
drift along anyhow'. So-and-so's daughter is married; the
rest are still ''pon the stream'. Someone else had a nice
little 'tenement', and brought up ten children ''pon the
ground'.

Note *however*, delimiting a very qualifying clause in a
narrative.

'Like Hocken's ducks – hadn' no meat nor feather'.

Bray's tale of an old lady at Bodmin who kept a general
shop. Having a money dispute with someone, which
culminated in a successful lawsuit, she composed a set of
satirical verses and distributed them by having them
printed on the papers in which she wrapped the tea.

The fine weather at the beginning of autumn is known in
Bodmin as 'St Pratt's little summer'. [St Pratt frequented
Blisland.]

So-and-so going to be a road-surveyor: 'Why, he never
crawled through a cunderd [conduit] in his life'.

Some men were digging a hole in the ground, when a
discussion arose as to what was to be done with the stuff
taken out. So-and-so suggested the digging of another pit
to put it in. This may be taken as a typical Cornish bull,
differing from the Irish breed in being less vivacious,
simple – simple, indeed, to the point of stupidity.

Of a farmer in the early board-school days who was dead
against the education of hinds. All they wanted to know

*Regular eighteenth-century usage in standard English.

was the time to come to work; he could tell them the time to leave off.

The Christmas *stock* (or *mock* or *mott*), drawn to the house by a yoke of bullocks. On the same day, five men would be set to work cutting and binding ash-faggots. What would the modern farmer say, if he were asked to pay a day's wages to five men for the sake of a Christmas jollification? A piece of the stock, about the size of a box-hat, was saved and used to kindle the fire on the following Christmas Day, 'to "carr" the fire from year to year', as R.R. puts it.

A farmer in the Mawgan area whose name was Read. He was elderly, and a glutton for work. When old, he would hoe mangolds as long as he could walk, and then he would go down on hands and knees and crawl, still hoeing. When he got up, he would be 'plaistered' with earth from head to foot, as Reuben has seen him scores of times. R. pronounces *plaister* in this way, as written.

Of a 'gentleman' out Bodmin way, whose chief delight was riding in a crowded market bus. The pleasure consisted in holding a young woman on his knees, or sitting on hers, or being squeezed between two damsels. He would drive out a few miles, dismiss the man with the trap, and wait for the bus.

Another Cornish bull: Father from his bedroom: 'Hold your noise maidens! Don't 'ee know I'm upstairs sleeping?'

I have heard that you can always tell a Cornishman by this: that when he is listening to a statement, he indicates his continued attention by a breath indrawn through half-closed lips. After my attention had been drawn to this, I noted it continually in Reuben Rosevear and Tom Eplett.

[But Lee adds a later note:] It is found also in Devon and Somerset.

Note R.R.'s 'I'd better lace boots' – the only part of the morning *toilette* to be particularised. Does this point, as the absence of the spade in Cornwall is said to do, to a time when rural Cornwall went barefooted? There is still something of a ritual in the putting on of R.'s boots: chair pulled out near fire; boots fetched by missus, etc. Then (it is when he goes out driving a party, or to market) the dicky, collar and necktie are taken from the dresser and adjusted by Mrs Rosevear.

Of pig-killing in Mawgan in the old saltless days, the custom of dividing the carcase among the neighbours, on the understanding that the joint which is selected is to be returned at a future killing. This is still done here with the parts which are not salted, the roasting joints. Someone says he doesn't mind receiving his allotted part, but when it comes in repayment, he laments the pretty little hole it makes in the carcase. During the fattening of the pig, interested neighbours save their potato peelings, etc., and bring them to assist in the process. In recompense they expect a slice of ham, some fry, or other tit-bit. The same selfish character, when killing-time was at hand, used to recommend his missus to fall out with these folk, so that the question of repayment might not be raised. It is the wife's job to supply a 'furnace' (i.e. a furnace pan) full of hot water for the scalding.

There is talk, in Mawgan, of Jan Jacobs of Polruan, who had a 'black heart', which made it dangerous, it seems, to cross or quarrel with him. A neighbouring old woman, a 'witch', was mortally afraid of him; for it appears that the possession of a black heart puts you high in the hierarchy of Satan. She even consulted him in fear and trembling when things went wrong. Her donkey falling ill, he told her to get a pail of blacksmith's ashes, the soot or 'black dew of the forge', mix it with water, and administer. The donkey recovered. Then she lost him; gipsies were suspected. Could Jan help her? Jan must first consult his book. Yes, the donkey would come back; he could see him trotting homewards in the pages of his book; in four days' time he would be at her door. And in four days' time, sure enough, the donkey trotted down the street, descended the cellar steps, and put his head in over the half-hatch. Jan made a wager that he would go into the church tower without a light at midnight and bring out a skull. A joker secreted himself beforehand. Jan enters, gropes around, finds a skull, a fine big one, round and 'clane', will do very well. As he departs, a hollow voice exclaims 'That's mine'. 'Beg pardon, sir, I'm sure,' says Jan, drops the skull, and fumbles for another. He takes one, not so big, but a tidy li'll skull, do very well. Again the hollow voice: 'That's mine!' 'Damn 'ee for a liar,' says Jan. 'Never had but one in your life!'

Somebody's affairs, in Mawgan, are in a parlous state. Says one farmer: 'I'll eat beef in his barn before very long', referring to the custom of providing luncheons for buyers at auction sales.

They have been testing the strain of the new bridge across the 'river' at Mawgan. Will it bear the steam-roller? One district councillor suggests: 'Man with wooden leg – hundredweight to the square inch.'

October 3rd. Gorran Haven again. This is the Cornwall of

15. Gorran, 1909

my youth, the Cornwall of neighbourly seas and seaweed smells and fuchsia crowding over whitewashed porches and shouting seagulls. Coming in the wagonette from St Austell were a middle-aged countryman, and two young women, one married, the other (I judged) a housemaid, home for a holiday. Sam Kitto, the handsome driver, flirting with the last: head slewed round all the while, rarely a perfunctory glance at the road. Neighbourly views exchanged and discussed; who dead, who married, who courting. Of a girl engaged six years and then thrown over; a good girl, would make an excellent wife (look how she helps her mother), yet what chance has she now? Young men are shy of jilted maidens. Another girl, a flirt; her latest sweetheart has just suffered the usual fate. She won't have any difficulty in finding another. All of which is said to prove that there is no sense in males.

Withy plantations on the cliffs and in the valley hereabouts. Fishermen *teal* their own withies for the rims, etc. of the crab-pots. The stouter withies for the framework they have to walk five miles to fetch. Farmers are reluctant to supply them, as they trample hedges and leave gaps for cattle when fetching their supplies.

Contrast the hierarchy of society in the farming districts with the republican equality of these little fishing villages.

Surnames hereabouts: Whetter, Martyn, Guy, Pill, Dadda. Note that the name Lanyon is accented on the last syllable.

'Fine Easter; wet Gorran Feast', which occurs a fortnight later. 'The maidens of Gorran, on Feast Day, pull at your coat, three or four of 'em to wance, with "Ben't 'ee going to treat us?" And all the rest of the year they won't so much as look at 'ee.'

I am told in Gorran of an old woman, not long dead, a direct inheritor of the tradition of old Cornish 'drolls'. She would come to your door and improvise a whole string of rhymes about yourself and others in the room. My informant repeated some of her verses, referring to the Crimean War.

In the train back to Letchworth, I was told of a Cornish driver who was congratulated by his fare on his obligingness and affability. 'My father,' said he, 'drove a trap before me, and he used to say, "There's more flies catched with treacle than with vinegar".'*

*An alternative phrase, which I have heard, is 'Oil is cheaper than sandpaper'.

[In 1908, Charles Lee comes to Cornwall for a holiday, staying at Mawgan and also at Gorran Haven. At Mawgan he met his old friend Reuben Rosevear; and also one Bray, formerly carpenter and attendant at Bodmin Asylum: Bray had J.T. Blight* (author of *Ancient Cornish Crosses*) in his charge.]

Blight 'queer', but not deserving confinement. B. told Bray that the best way to decipher an ancient inscription was to look at it by candle-light.

*J.T. Blight (1835–1911) was also the author of *A Week at the Land's End*. See John Michell, *A Short Life at the Land's End: J.T. Blight FSA, Artist* (of Penzance). Bath, 1977.

The last forty years of Blight's life were spent at the County Asylum, Bodmin.